MARRIAGE

ALSO BY RICK CHAFE

The Secret Mask
Shakespeare's Dog
Strike! The Musical (with Danny Schur)

MARRIAGE:
A DEMOLITION IN TWO ACTS

RICK CHAFE

PLAYWRIGHTS CANADA PRESS
TORONTO

For professional or amateur production rights, please contact:
Michael Petrasek, Kensington Literary Representation
34 St. Andrew Street, Toronto, ON M5T 1K6
416.848.9648 :: kensingtonlit@rogers.com

LIBRARY AND ARCHIVES CANADA CATALOGUING IN PUBLICATION
Title: Marriage : a demolition in two acts / Rick Chafe.
Names: Chafe, Rick, author.
Description: First edition. | A play.
Identifiers: Canadiana (print) 20190082542 | Canadiana (ebook) 20190082550
| ISBN 9781770919969 (softcover) | ISBN 9781770919976 (PDF)
| ISBN 9781770919983 (EPUB) | ISBN 9781770919990 (Kindle)
Classification: LCC PS8555.H265 M37 2019 | DDC C812/.6—dc23

Playwrights Canada Press acknowledges that we operate on land, which, for thousands of years, has been the traditional territories of the Mississaugas of the Credit First Nation, Huron-Wendat, Anishinaabe, Métis, and Haudenosaunee peoples. Today, this meeting place is home to many Indigenous peoples from across Turtle Island and we are grateful to have the opportunity to work and play here.

We acknowledge the financial support of the Canada Council for the Arts—which last year invested $153 million to bring the arts to Canadians throughout the country—the Ontario Arts Council (OAC), Ontario Creates, and the Government of Canada for our publishing activities.

 Canada Council Conseil des arts
for the Arts du Canada

 ONTARIO ARTS COUNCIL
CONSEIL DES ARTS DE L'ONTARIO
an Ontario government agency
un organisme du gouvernement de l'Ontario

 Canada

 ONTARIO | ONTARIO
CREATES | CRÉATIF

For Martine with love.

Marriage: A Demolition in Two Acts premiered on March 17, 2016, at Prairie Theatre Exchange, Winnipeg, with the following cast and creative team:

Wayne: Tom Anniko
Julie: Marina Stephenson Kerr
John: Justin Otto
Maggie: Erin McGrath

Director: Robert Metcalfe
Set and Costume Design: Brian Perchaluk
Lighting Design: Scott Henderson
Music and Sound Design: Greg Lowe
Stage Manager: Melissa Novecosky

CHARACTERS

Wayne, fifty-seven
Julie, fifty-five
John, twenty-four
Maggie, twenty-four

The play is written to be current for 2019, but productions may choose to update the technology, prices, and pop culture references, depending how the referenced events play out in the future. This version is set in Winnipeg, but local references may be changed to suit the locale of the production.

ACT ONE
SCENE ONE

A very small kitchen with room to play out in a dining and/or living room, and an indication of a front door exit and front walkway. WAYNE, *fifty-seven, enters, followed by* JOHN, *twenty-four, carrying a clipboard.*

WAYNE: So, here it is.

JOHN: That's . . . wow. That's a small kitchen.

WAYNE: Yup. But that's not the problem.

JOHN: No, small kitchens can be really nice.

WAYNE: I think so, but who am I?

JOHN: Yeah. What?

WAYNE: The problem is the dishwasher.

JOHN: Right. Which is where?

WAYNE: There isn't one.

JOHN: No dishwasher?

WAYNE: Nope.

JOHN: Wow. You just moved in?

WAYNE: Thirty years ago. So where do we put it?

JOHN: Where?

WAYNE: Yeah.

JOHN: Well, you could take out those two banks of drawers?

WAYNE: Nope.

JOHN: Can you do without the pantry?

WAYNE: Tried that, wouldn't fly.

JOHN: Um. Maybe get one of those portable dishwashers on wheels?

WAYNE: Suggested that. It was a two-hour fight.

JOHN: Unless you're ripping out all these counters and starting again?

WAYNE: Yup. Just to get a dishwasher.

JOHN: Gotcha. That's a pretty expensive dishwasher.

WAYNE: Exactly. So if we can keep costs down, that'd be a good thing.

JOHN: I'm your man.

JOHN takes out his phone, selects an app.

Okay if I grab some measurements?

WAYNE: Whatever you need. But here's the thing—

JOHN stands in the centre of the kitchen, points the phone at a wall and begins turning in a circle, stopping a moment at each corner and doorway to line up a marker on the screen.

What are you doing?

JOHN: Measuring.

WAYNE: You're kidding.

JOHN: My dad showed me this. Gets everything, even the doors.

He holds his phone up for WAYNE.

There's your floor plan.

WAYNE: Wow.

JOHN: Isn't that great?

WAYNE: Nice!

JOHN: Right? What were you going to say?

WAYNE: Yeah—so she'll be home any minute and the thing is—

JOHN: *(typing in a note)* Sorry, I started with the north wall, right?

WAYNE: South wall.

JOHN: Mmm, north.

WAYNE: That's south.

JOHN: Okay. "South" wall . . .

WAYNE: *(helping out)* South, north, east, west.

JOHN: You're calling that east?

WAYNE: It *is* east.

JOHN: *(typing in a note)* Okay, we're calling it the east wall. I'm good with that.

WAYNE: That's east.

JOHN: Sure. I drove here south on Pembina, but whatever. Just saying.

WAYNE: Yeah, but Pembina bends because the river bends so all the streets off Pembina bend and then they bend some more and I've lived here for thirty years, that's east.

JOHN: I'm sorry. I'm totally sorry. I get that way. You're the customer.

WAYNE: All right. Now here's the thing—

JULIE, fifty-five, wife of WAYNE, enters the house, unseen from the kitchen.

JULIE: *(calling)* Hellooo?

WAYNE: Oh crap.

JULIE: *(calling)* Hi, honey.

WAYNE: *(to JOHN, quickly)* Remember this: you work for me, not for her, got it?

JOHN: What?

JULIE: Helloo?

WAYNE: Just keep that thought—

(calling) We're in here.

    JULIE enters the kitchen, coat still on.

JULIE: Who's we?

(to JOHN) Hi!

JOHN: Hi!

WAYNE: John, Julie.

JULIE: Hi, John. Uh, what are you doing here?

WAYNE: John's here to give us a quote on the kitchen.

JULIE: A quote?

WAYNE: A quote.

JULIE: Are you serious?

WAYNE: Look at my face.

JULIE: But this is . . . My god. I can't believe this.

WAYNE: You said you wanted a kitchen.

JULIE: I've been saying I wanted a kitchen for . . . ho ho ho! Looong time.

WAYNE: And I said I'd start calling contractors.

JULIE: It's just— Wow! You really did!

WAYNE: Overreacting, honey.

JULIE: So, John—John?

JOHN: Yup?

JULIE: What part do you do?

JOHN: All of it.

JULIE: You build entire kitchens?

JOHN: Sure.

JULIE: Sorry, I'm . . . I'm kind of in shock here. You look kind of . . . Well, great! Good for you! Give me two seconds—

She goes to hang up her coat.

WAYNE: *(quickly and quietly)* Whatever she wants, we're not giving it to her, all right?

JOHN: What?

WAYNE: The kitchen she wants would cost half a million dollars. If you quote me half a million, you don't get the job—got it?

JOHN: Right—so how do we—

JULIE: *(offstage)* Okaaay!

WAYNE: Here we go.

> *JULIE returns.*

JULIE: John? How much?

JOHN: How much?

JULIE: I'm kidding. I just wanted Wayne to know right from the start—honey, I appreciate you doing this, and I'm thinking about the money.

WAYNE: Well, that's very impressive.

JULIE: So where have we got to?

> *JOHN, uncertain, checks with WAYNE.*

JOHN: Uh, we've measured the room?

WAYNE: Yes we have.

JULIE: Okay then. Just roughly, if we replaced all the cabinets you see here with, say, mid-to-upper-line Ikea, what would you say we're looking at?

JOHN: Well . . .

WAYNE: Maybe you could get back to us with that, John?

JOHN: Right.

JULIE: Sweetheart, I'm just asking for a rough idea.

WAYNE: The range on these things is huge, honey, there're so many variables—

JULIE: I know there're variables.

WAYNE: So how can he know off the top of his head?

JULIE: He must have a *rough* idea, right, John?

JOHN: Well . . . The last kitchen I did was a little bigger than this—

JULIE: *Every* kitchen is bigger than this.

JOHN: And those were pretty nice cabinets—

JULIE: We don't want cheap.

WAYNE: Economical would be good.

JULIE: John, how much were they?

JOHN: They, were . . .

JOHN *glances at* WAYNE. WAYNE *shrugs helplessly.*

. . . twenty-five thousand dollars. But—

WAYNE: *Twenty-five thousand—?*

JULIE: Not as bad as I thought. That gives us some room. Now, flooring—

WAYNE: We are not buying twenty-five-thousand-dollar cabinets, just get it out of your head.

JULIE: Honey, relax. This *is* going to cost money.

WAYNE: Don't start with the patronizing—

JULIE: I'm sorry. You called a contractor. You're doing very well. I know this hurts.

WAYNE: *(a warning)* Julie—

JULIE: *(to WAYNE)* Sorry. John. You look about twelve years old. Have you really done this before?

JOHN: What? Yes!

JULIE: Great, that's wonderful. But it would be just like my husband to look for the cheapest contractor in the city. That's not you, right?

JOHN: That's not— No! I think I'm pretty reasonable, but—

JULIE: Good! Now, obviously, we're tearing everything out and starting from scratch. We're agreed on that much, right?

WAYNE: We're not agreed on anything—we haven't actually talked about any of this.

JULIE: I have said it at least a million times. I guess maybe you weren't listening. For instance, John, this work triangle doesn't work. Correct?

JOHN: Uh, work triangle, yeah—

JULIE: The stove is idiotic there, there's no counter space beside the sink, the fridge next to the window is blocking all the energy, we need it moved.

JOHN: Right. Where?

JULIE: Africa. Anywhere, just not where it is. New cabinets, about double as many as we have now.

JOHN: *Double?*

JULIE: I don't know how, I'm just saying this kitchen is impossible. We want two decent-size new windows and a full patio-door entrance onto the deck.

JOHN: What deck?

JULIE: Exactly. And I hate the dining room door here, it has to move.

JOHN: Move to . . . ?

JULIE: I don't know. You're doing the drawings, just show us something. You can draw, right?

JOHN: Sure.

JOHN *grabs his pad and pencil.*

WAYNE: Oh for god sakes, would you give him a break?

JULIE: What, he has his pencil, he can do a drawing—

WAYNE: How can he possibly draw what you're talking about?

JULIE: Give him some credit, you think he can't give us a professional drawing?

JOHN: No, I can—

WAYNE: Of course he can't, he's twelve years old!

JULIE: Then why didn't you call a real contractor?

WAYNE: I didn't know how old he was! I just had to get a contractor of my own before you started bringing in *your* contractors!

JULIE: Why?

WAYNE: Ammunition!

JULIE: Oh my god.

WAYNE: My reasonable quote to fight your sky's the limit quote!

JOHN *takes out his phone.*

JOHN: Do you mind if I—?

JULIE: Wayne, this is no way to do things.

WAYNE: It's the only way! I've been living with you for thirty years, believe me, I'm an expert!

JULIE: We're never going to do this kitchen, are we?

WAYNE: John, forget it. Julie and I will have a calm and rational discussion and call you sometime in the next century.

JOHN: *(on phone)* Hi.
Could use a little—
No, please, really. I'm really sorry. Totally, totally sorry.
So totally. Just—
I know.
I know.
I know. But you are more awesome than I could ever deserve and just come on inside, please please please?
Yee-*ahhh*.
Okay, love you.

JOHN hangs up.

Do you mind if I call in my business associate for a consultation?

The doorbell rings. JULIE *goes to answer it . . .*

WAYNE: Business associate?

. . . but MAGGIE's *already in.*

MAGGIE: Hi. Maggie.

JULIE: Oh, another one.

MAGGIE: Well—yes! Here's my card.

MAGGIE hands JULIE a card, then sees WAYNE.

Oh! And co-inhabitant. Maggie.

She hands WAYNE a card.

WAYNE: Wonderful.

MAGGIE: And . . . ?

She looks at JOHN, who is beaming at her.

Our clients' names?

JOHN: Right!

JOHN flips through his notepad.

Wayne! And . . . Crap—

JULIE: Julie. *(reading the card)* You sell green cleaning products.

MAGGIE: Green cleaning products—

MAGGIE turns the card around for JULIE.

—and I have a degree in design and programming. My first line of women's clothing including yoga outfits, a men's line launching next month, also website design and phone apps. I'm working on recycled-material outdoor furniture—but my passion? Is kitchens.

JULIE and WAYNE are looking doubtful.

You saw John's website, right?

WAYNE: I tore his number off the bulletin board at the Save All Foods.

JOHN: I *told* you!

MAGGIE: Wonderful. *(recovering)* So! Who wants to start?

JULIE: Oh, I'm all warmed up.

WAYNE: *(to JOHN)* Stand back.

JULIE: There's all the chipped paint. The unremovable stains. The window that won't open. The cupboard doors that will. Not. Close. The vinyl flooring that somehow peels up at every corner in synchronization. The bare lightbulb because a glass shade was shattered twenty years ago by a ten-year-old with a hockey stick and never replaced. The missing trim on the doorway, the added shelving that looks like it was cut with a hatchet, three missing cupboard handles, these bloody ugly drawer pulls!

WAYNE: *(simultaneously quietly parodying)* "These bloody ugly drawer pulls!"

MAGGIE: Those are tragic.

JULIE: And the size of this counter. When you make a piece of toast on this counter you have to take it to the dining room to butter it. I'm ashamed to tell you this but there is mould under the sink.

MAGGIE: Julie, this ain't my first rodeo.

WAYNE: I like the mould. It kind of grows on you.

JULIE: Oh god, shut him up! Please shut him up!

MAGGIE: Julie—

JULIE: How are the two of us still together? You are right. You are right.

WAYNE: I don't think she was asking that.

Without turning, MAGGIE *holds up her index finger to silence* WAYNE.

MAGGIE: Julie, forget about *this* kitchen. We're ripping it out, it's gone. Just tell me about your dream kitchen.

Well-trained, JOHN *pulls out his phone, ready to record.*

WAYNE: Why don't we pause for a breather here—

MAGGIE: Tst!

She cues JOHN *and he points the phone's camera at* JULIE.

Pause.

JULIE: I don't think subway tiles are too much to ask, do you?

MAGGIE: Not too much at all.

WAYNE: I can do subway tiles for you, honey. I have always said I can make you a backsplash.

JULIE: *(to* WAYNE*)* And it is *where?*

(back to MAGGIE*)* Decent cabinets.

MAGGIE: That's a given.

JULIE: With *usable* space. And a special one, a huge one, with an enormous pull-out drawer just for pots.

MAGGIE: You'll want at least two of those.

JULIE: *Three* huge pot drawers. Or one of those screens that hangs down from the ceiling with hooks for pots and pans.

MAGGIE: Talk to me about appliances.

JULIE: A new fridge, obviously.

MAGGIE: God, yes.

JULIE: Stove.

MAGGIE: Have you thought about a steam oven?

JULIE: Ohhh yes.

WAYNE: What the hell is a steam oven?

MAGGIE: Combi-steam?

JULIE: You're imagining someone else's life.

MAGGIE: Let it out. I'm seeing a matching convection oven.

JULIE: Where's the room for it?

MAGGIE: We'll find it.

WAYNE: *(to JOHN)* What in god's name is going on?

JOHN *shrugs, keeps filming.*

JULIE: Okay. Counter space for a six-slice toaster, food processor, espresso machine—we can talk about brands—

MAGGIE: Brands are my life.

JULIE: I would like drawers that slide nicely, all the way out, and have that smooth, *glidey* feeling, and then they kind of slow to a perfect halt even if you slam them?

MAGGIE: We can do that with cupboard doors too.

JULIE: Oh, but leave me one that slams. I *like* to slam a good cupboard door now and then.

MAGGIE: You go!

JULIE: And a huge new window, that whole wall, somehow, with a big, deep farmhouse double sink and—the water spout turny things, on the sink, the, the, whadyacallit—

JOHN: Faucets?

JULIE: Yes, faucets, thank you.

JOHN: My mom has those senior moments too.

Pause.

MAGGIE: *(saving it)* Countertops.

JULIE: Granite.

MAGGIE: Cement?

JULIE: No-oo!

MAGGIE: Yee-es! Or marble? Quartz? Wood-grained Formica—backlit?

JULIE: Really?

MAGGIE: Floors?

JULIE: Cork.

MAGGIE: Stone?

JULIE: Too cold.

MAGGIE: Hot water pipes underneath.

JULIE: Oh my god.

MAGGIE: Better than sex.

JULIE: For me, maybe.

MAGGIE: Julie, I know exactly what you want. I just have to design *my* dream kitchen and I already know you'll love it.

WAYNE: Okay, hold it—

MAGGIE: AND Wayne, I understand there is a financial pressure involved here that I will keep right here, in my frontal lobe, at all moments of the design process.

WAYNE: Uh-huh.

MAGGIE: I cannot wait to start on this, no obligation. I'm going to deliver preliminary drawings and a quote in three days, just as a starting place, anything you're unhappy with can be changed. May we proceed?

Pause. JULIE looks at WAYNE. WAYNE makes a "don't look at me!" gesture.

JULIE: *(to MAGGIE)* All right. Start designing.

MAGGIE: All I need is your best guess at the budget you want me to work with.

JULIE: Fifty thousand.

WAYNE: *(following closely)* Ten thousand.

Beat.

MAGGIE: Should we try that again?

JULIE: Forty-five thousand.

WAYNE: Fifteen thousand.

MAGGIE: Good. Good. Let's go, John.

JULIE: We could probably tighten that range a little. Couldn't we, Wayne.

WAYNE: No, we could not.

MAGGIE: *(sweetly)* No. No no no no no.

(less sweetly) John? Get in the truck.

MAGGIE exits towards the front door.

JOHN: *(to JULIE)* Is your living room busy for a moment?

JULIE: All yours.

JOHN: *(calling after)* Mags? Quick meeting?

JOHN follows MAGGIE.

WAYNE: Kids, eh? Were we ever that young?

JULIE: What is wrong with you?

WAYNE: Me?

JULIE: This is not a marriage. This is not what married people do.

WAYNE: Fighting over a kitchen reno? Relax, we're normal.

JULIE: It's not the kitchen, Wayne. It's you. People always say to me, what's wrong with your husband, and I laugh and say, that's just Wayne. But this is serious. You have a serious problem.

WAYNE: There's no problem, we'll just call another contractor.

JULIE: You will never let this kitchen be renovated. You used to be just cheap, but this is a whole new level.

WAYNE: Oh come on.

JULIE: Wayne, you have become terrified of life.

WAYNE: I am not terrified of life.

JULIE: Then what is it? You don't even leave the house anymore.

WAYNE: I went to the store this morning.

JULIE: In a car. And you got out, paid, got back in, drove home. Back to the TV, back to the couch, back to the same clothes, the same shoes, the same food, the beer, the Internet—oh my god, how can you stand yourself?

WAYNE: Having routines is not a crime.

JULIE: Is it a gambling addiction?

WAYNE: No!

JULIE: Is it porn?

WAYNE: *No!*

JULIE: Why not? Any healthy person living the way you do would have a porn addiction by now! Is there a single drop of passion left in your veins?

WAYNE: This isn't about passion! This is about you spending our retirement fund!

JULIE: Oh god, Wayne!

WAYNE: It's true! We're hemorrhaging money. We'll be broke in ten years.

JULIE: We won't be broke and I don't care if we are! I don't want to save every cent for when we're old, I want to spend some while we're young enough to enjoy it!

WAYNE: And I just want a little say in how we pour our money down the drain.

JULIE: You want a say? Then get a job.

WAYNE: Oh. Good.

JULIE: Oh crapolla . . .

WAYNE: No, game on, let's go—

JULIE: I apologize for mentioning the situation—

WAYNE: Do you know how many—

JULIE: *(overlapping)* Yes I do—

WAYNE: *(overlapping)* —job applications I put in—

JULIE: *(overlapping)* Forty-seven.

WAYNE: *(overlapping)* Forty-seven. I think I've established very well that no one wants me—

JULIE: Please, let's not have this discussion—

WAYNE: Granted, I've been looking only within my professional field. Maybe it's time I strolled down to Walmart—

JULIE: *(overlapping)* Nobody's asking you to go to Walmart—

WAYNE: —stick my name in—

JULIE: *(overlapping)* —I'm sorry, I'm very sorry, it slipped out—

WAYNE: *(overlapping)* —see if they need any greeters!

JULIE: *(blurting)* We need a marriage counsellor!

WAYNE: What?

JULIE: Marriage counselling. We're the reason it exists. We need it.

WAYNE: Why? We're fine.

JULIE: My god, Wayne, we're not fine! We survived the kids for what, to kill each other? I want to live again. I want to go out more than once a month; I want to do all the travelling we planned on; I want to buy things without an argument; I want to quit my job—I am so sick of my job. I might want to retire early, Wayne, like any second now.

WAYNE: If you retire, we are seriously screwed.

JULIE: You see? You'd be happy with the way things are for the rest of your life and I can't stand the way things are for one more second and I don't think we can even talk about it without a professional.

WAYNE: We don't need a professional. We can do this—we are capable of compromise.

JULIE: I am compromising, Wayne. I wanted so much more out of this marriage than this, my list was very very long. This kitchen is my compromise. That's what I'm settling for. You promised me a kitchen; this is my release valve to let the pressure off. Give me my kitchen or I am going to blow. I can feel it and it won't be pretty.

WAYNE: Okay, calm now—

JULIE: Not calming, not calming at all. I can't stand what we've become. Is this all you expected to be, Wayne? Is this really us?

WAYNE: No, it is not.

JULIE: We're good people, we worked hard our whole lives. Is this what we deserved?

WAYNE: No.

JULIE: This isn't good enough, but our lives are not over. We still have good years together. Right?

WAYNE: Do we?

JULIE: What?

WAYNE: What if? Just think about it. What if?

JULIE: What is this? Just say it.

WAYNE: If we went broke. Would we still be together if we didn't have any money?

JULIE: Wayne— Sweetheart . . . Is that what you're worried about?

WAYNE: Only at night. And then in the day.

JULIE: Sweetheart, we'll be okay.

WAYNE: I just don't know anymore. What is there we can really count on?

JULIE: On us, sweetheart. We can count on us. We've made it thirty years and, after everything, we're still together. And we have savings, we have investments, we have my job, and even if disaster ever struck, we could sell the house and be fine, right?

WAYNE: Right . . .

JULIE: So can we please take this one little risk?

Beat.

WAYNE: Can you do this kitchen without going crazy?

JULIE: I can do the most reasonable and thrifty kitchen humanly possible. Can you hold back from adding the cost of every screw on a calculator?

WAYNE: I believe I can do that.

JULIE: Okay.

WAYNE: Okay.

JULIE: Now what do we do with those two?

Lights out on the kitchen. Lights up on the living room.

JOHN: They are going to crack.

MAGGIE: I don't care. I don't want anything to do with them.

JOHN: Mags, it's not just a fence or a back deck, it's a whole kitchen—

MAGGIE: No, they're just like every other sad old couple in this city. They'll want fifty thousand dollars worth of value for ten. They have a chance to actually help two promising young people get a toe in the door, and first chance they get they will slam it again and break our feet. They are bad news, screw them, let's get out of here.

JOHN: Except—

MAGGIE: And I wouldn't even care except you were an hour late picking me up.

JOHN: And I am so sorry about that—

MAGGIE: I could have taken a bus if you'd called me—

JOHN: I know, but my phone died—

MAGGIE: Plus you didn't even come home last night—

JOHN: Because I was kind of wrapped up in this thing—

MAGGIE: Except you're *always* wrapped up in a thing, and I know what I'm sounding like but I'm getting really freaked out over all the student loans and I don't want to go back to telemarketing and I don't want you driving for Uber Eats and I don't care, stay out all night, I don't own you, but when I can't get hold of you, like ever, so that I missed a real meeting where I could have sold real product to a real company—

JOHN: I know, I totally know—

MAGGIE: Instead of wasting our time playing house with the walking dead—

JOHN: And I'm going to tell you why—

MAGGIE: Good. Can't wait. Go tell them we'll send a quote and mention that they should hurry up and die. Let's go.

JOHN: I got the land.

She stops. Turns.

MAGGIE: What land?

JOHN: Our land.

MAGGIE: The corner lot.

JOHN: Yup.

MAGGIE: The corner lot with the baby cypress trees.

JOHN: Yeah.

MAGGIE: What do you mean you got it?

JOHN: The municipality had a tax sale. I waited outside the office all night so I could be first in line this morning. I was going to wait to surprise you tonight.

MAGGIE: How much . . . ?

JOHN: The developer went bankrupt. They sold off fourteen parcels for totally practically nothing.

MAGGIE: How much?

JOHN: Twenty-five thou.

MAGGIE: *Twenty-five thousand?*

JOHN: Yeah!

MAGGIE: Where did you get twenty-five thousand?

JOHN: On the Visa.

MAGGIE: You're maxed on the Visa.

JOHN: I got a MasterCard to put the minimum on the Visa.

MAGGIE: That's not even close.

JOHN: Okay, I borrowed it from my mom, but I ordered a Citibank and a Capital One and another one I can't remember so I can pay her back just about the whole thing.

MAGGIE: You'll never get another card now.

JOHN: But you've got a card.

MAGGIE: John, no—lending each other money is the kiss of death.

JOHN: Except it's not lending if we were a married couple.

JOHN goes down on one knee.

MAGGIE: Oh crap.

JOHN: A married couple who own a corner lot with baby cypress trees on it.

MAGGIE: John, we just moved in together.

JOHN: I know, but isn't it a cool engagement present?

MAGGIE: You're not even doing it right. You're supposed to have a ring.

JOHN: Okay, I'll get one more card and I can get a ring. But I thought we could just drive out to our land tonight and stick our fingers in the ground to make it official. For now.

MAGGIE: The ground is frozen, stupid.

JOHN: I've got a blowtorch in the truck.

MAGGIE: John . . . I love the engagement gift. I love the baby cypress trees.

JOHN: And we can build our little house.

MAGGIE: And I love our little house. But that's a someday plan, not a today plan. We have to wait until we know.

JOHN: I don't need to wait. I love you, Mags.

MAGGIE: I love you too, John. I really do.

JOHN: I already know I'm going to love you forever.

MAGGIE: I know, it's just . . . What if we get picked?

JOHN: Then we sell the land and we're the happiest people on the planet.

MAGGIE: What if one of us gets picked. And the other doesn't?

JOHN: Then it's a long-distance love affair and I'm still good with that.

MAGGIE: It's a really, really long distance.

JOHN: Mags, I know we said everything's gotta be a someday plan for now. But twenty-five thousand for our corner lot? That's a today plan.

MAGGIE: I know, but still—

JOHN: We could sell it tomorrow and make a killing.

MAGGIE: Okay, definitely true.

JOHN: I wasn't even going to mention any of this until tonight, and no pressure, honest, except here's the chance to make some of the twenty-five thousand now and actually *pay* for the land and maybe even start building our little house not someday but today—

She's about to speak, but he stops her.

And if it's totally, no way, ever going to happen, it's okay, I can get the whole twenty-five back. But that's only until next Friday. So the thing is, if you really, really don't want to marry me, I kind of need you to say so by next Friday, before noon. Okay?

Pause. MAGGIE *nods her head.*

Yes, you'll marry me?

MAGGIE *cocks her head—"not saying that."*

Yes, you'll tell me by next Friday?

MAGGIE *nods her head.*

But just in case . . .

MAGGIE: Let's go get the money?

They both nod happily and kiss.

Lights up on WAYNE *and* JULIE *in the kitchen.*

WAYNE: Children! Come on back in, we've decided to play nice!

MAGGIE and JOHN break their kiss and head back into the kitchen.

MAGGIE: Julie and Wayne. Forget the budget, I'm going to draw the kitchen you need. And when you see it, we can just add or subtract features until we find a price you're happy with. How's that?

WAYNE: We can do better than that. My love and I have decided on one single number.

WAYNE and JULIE *look at each other.*

JULIE: *(simultaneously)* Thirty thousand.

WAYNE: *(simultaneously)* Thirty thousand.

MAGGIE: Perfect. John?

JOHN: I think we could do something with that.

WAYNE: Now just to be clear. We didn't ask for a designer. We're not paying a designer fee.

Beat.

MAGGIE: *(burying the anger)* For you? Included.

WAYNE: And I'm not seeing a lot of experience here, which means we're taking a pretty big risk. So *if* we decide to go with you, we're not putting any more than twenty percent up front.

JOHN: We can—wow—do that somehow, can't we, Mags?

MAGGIE: Of course we can, on *fifty* percent up front.

WAYNE: I'm sure you could, but it's twenty.

MAGGIE: That's really out of the question.

JOHN: *(overlapping)* We can make that work.

JULIE: And . . . so we all get the best value out of this, John, Wayne is going to work with you.

JOHN & WAYNE: *What?*

JULIE: *(to JOHN)* He has a ton of experience. He renovated half this house.

JOHN: I have my own guy I call in—

WAYNE: No no no no no no no—

MAGGIE: This is not possible; this is a total deal breaker—

JULIE: This has no effect on your earnings—the budget remains the same. We're supplying Wayne's labour. Your costs stay low and we end up with more kitchen for our money.

WAYNE: No no no no—

JULIE: *(to WAYNE)* You need a project, honey. You need to get involved in the world again, and you *like* renovating.

WAYNE: I hate renovating!

MAGGIE: So he's like John's unpaid intern?

JULIE: Exactly. And his boss.

WAYNE: There is no way I'm doing any more renovating on this house ever again—

JOHN: There is no way this is going to work. This is a bad bad bad idea—

JULIE: *(to WAYNE)* It's exactly what you need.

(to JOHN) There are other contractors.

(to MAGGIE) Take it or leave it.

MAGGIE: I'm drawing it up based on thirty thousand. Twenty percent down.

JULIE: Subject to design approval—

MAGGIE: But, as we don't know Wayne's capability, there's no way we can estimate our labour if he's involved, so we'll have to charge by time. John's rate is thirty-five dollars an hour.

JULIE: Agreed, if and only if you can start Monday.

JOHN: I have two other jobs I kind of have to—

MAGGIE: *(shushing JOHN)* Shht!

(to JULIE) You're front of the line.

JULIE: Magnificent.

MAGGIE: And John and I have a dinner date. I'll call you in two days.

JULIE and WAYNE walk them to the front door.

JULIE: Can't wait.

MAGGIE and JOHN step out.

I know, saying yes is the hardest part.

WAYNE: Who said yes? We haven't even seen a proposal yet. Don't think this is a done deal. I am not even close to agreeing to this.

JULIE: Wayne, take a breath. We're building a kitchen, not the Great Wall of China. We'll be fine.

WAYNE: That's what you said about having children.

JULIE: You're right. I did.

JOHN and MAGGIE on the front steps.

JOHN: You're brilliant!

MAGGIE: And you just got a fifteen-dollar-an-hour raise!

JOHN: If we do this right, we'll pay off half the land.

MAGGIE: If we do this right, we'll pay off all the land and our little house.

They kiss. Lights out.

SCENE TWO

The stove and fridge have been moved into the dining room. A plastic sheet curtains off the kitchen door and drop cloths mark out short walkways from the kitchen to the fridge and to the front door. From the kitchen, boom box music is nearly drowned out by the sound of destruction.

The noise and music stop. WAYNE *emerges from the plastic curtain wearing a demolition suit, goggles, and respirator, filthy, carrying a sledgehammer. He coughs, heads for the fridge.* JOHN *steps out in the same outfit carrying a crowbar.*

JOHN: Great idea. I don't know why my dad always bangs out the old plaster and lath with a little claw hammer.

WAYNE *passes* JOHN *a beer from the fridge.*

WAYNE: Way faster with a sledgehammer, isn't it?

JOHN: No comparison.

They clink bottles, but JULIE *enters with three coffee travel mugs on a tray.*

JULIE: Morning, boys!

They instantly hide their beers.

WAYNE: Morning, sweetheart!

JOHN: Julie! Can you possibly be more lovely than yesterday?

JULIE: Coffee anyone?

JOHN: Oh, you know the answer!

> *WAYNE steps forward.*

WAYNE: Yes please!

JULIE: Drop cloth!

> *WAYNE jumps back.*

WAYNE: Sorry!

JULIE: *(to JOHN)* Sugar, sugar?

JOHN: Oh, honey, honey.

> *She giggles. He holds out his cup as she pours sugar into it from a dispenser, and he keeps tipping it up and up and up . . .*

Up up up up up up up— Perfect.

JULIE: Cream in your coffee?

JOHN: Not lately.

> *JULIE snorts at the obscenity.*

WAYNE: Okay, okay you two.

JOHN: *(sipping)* Dark roast today! Thank you!

WAYNE: *(sipping)* Nope, that's light roast.

JULIE: You're both right! I picked up a Keurig.

JOHN: Nice!

JULIE: I just thought it's crazy, everyone always running out to Starbucks to get it the way they like it, so this way we'll save some money and keep our nose to the grindstone.

WAYNE: Clever you!

> JOHN *lifts the kitchen curtain.*

JOHN: I'm gonna text Maggie, then do this last wall.

WAYNE: You made it twenty minutes yesterday without talking to her. Try for thirty today.

JOHN: 'Fraid that's impossible, Cap'n. Ma'am.

> JOHN *disappears into the kitchen again.*

JULIE: That boy, so sweet.

> JULIE *sits in a chair at the dining table and* WAYNE *pulls up a box on the drop cloth.*

WAYNE: You know, I am beginning to genuinely enjoy that kid.

JULIE: I know! You're beaming!

WAYNE: And his little sweetheart gal—

JULIE: I thought she was going to just be annoying—she's such a doll!

WAYNE: And she's kind of a genius.

JULIE opens up her "design book" and the two gaze at it with love.

JULIE: Beautiful.

WAYNE: It's perfect.

JULIE: This will be the most beautiful kitchen ever.

WAYNE: It will be.

JULIE: Receipts?

WAYNE opens up a notebook.

WAYNE: What have you got?

JULIE lays down the receipts.

JULIE: A little countertop oven, electric frying pan, and, ta da! a two-burner hot plate, all from the Goodwill! We have a temporary kitchen all for forty-seven bucks.

WAYNE marks it in the notebook.

WAYNE: Nicely done!

JULIE: And, my beautiful Keurig.

JULIE digs out her receipt.

A hundred and eighty-nine.

WAYNE: *A hundred and eighty-nine for a coffee maker?*

JULIE: That's what they cost.

WAYNE: Sorry, old habit.

> WAYNE *marks it in.*

Worth every penny.

JULIE: Plus the carafe.

WAYNE: A carafe? For what?

JULIE: It keeps the coffee hot.

WAYNE: It makes one cup at a time. Why do you need to keep it hot?

JULIE: If you use the bigger size K-Cup it makes a full carafe.

WAYNE: Our nice, cheap coffee maker already does that.

JULIE: *(carefully patient)* I will take back the Keurig and we can make do with the cheap one.

WAYNE: Sorry, question withdrawn. It's an excellent purchase, we're all going to love the Keurig.

> MAGGIE *enters.*

MAGGIE: Morning, everyone!

JULIE: Morning, beautiful. Coffee's right there—in the carafe.

MAGGIE: Nice!

JULIE: *(pointedly for* WAYNE's *benefit) Thank* you.

WAYNE: Anything else?

JULIE: Eight boxes of the Keurig cups and a recycle-a-cup—all on sale.

WAYNE: A . . . "recycle-a-cup"?

JULIE: It cuts the lid off the K-Cups so you can recycle them.

WAYNE: We have to buy a tool just to—

JULIE: *(cutting him off)* Please don't ask me that.

MAGGIE: It cuts the plastic rim off with the foil on it so you can recycle the rest of the cup.

WAYNE: What say we peel the foil off manually?

JULIE: You try that.

MAGGIE *laughs.*

WAYNE: I veto the recycle-a-cup.

MAGGIE *finally registers the controlled tension.*

MAGGIE: Oh.

JULIE: You want to use one of your three remaining vetoes over twelve dollars?

WAYNE: You're right. I withdraw the veto. What if, in good faith, you choose between these two fairly useless items?

JULIE: I object to the characterization of "useless."

WAYNE: I'm just asking to keep our eye on these smaller items so we don't blow the budget all to hell before we get to the big stuff.

JULIE: And we can do that if you get over this idea that a budget is carved in stone.

WAYNE: It *is* carved in stone.

JULIE: It's a flexible guideline to keep us in the ballpark.

WAYNE: The ballpark is all the money we have in the world.

JULIE: We're fine for money, and we built in a contingency fund, remember?

WAYNE: Which isn't there for convenience. It's there in case of horrible unanticipated emergencies.

JOHN enters.

JOHN: Guys?

JULIE: You're being ridiculous, *what* horrible emergencies?

WAYNE: I told you, the unanticipated ones!

JOHN: Wayne, you should maybe take a look at this?

WAYNE: Can it wait a minute?

JULIE: No, it can't. Take a break, Wayne. Go inhale some plaster dust.

WAYNE: Fine.

WAYNE and JOHN exit to kitchen.

MAGGIE: That was all over twelve bucks?

JULIE: Uh-huh.

MAGGIE: Does he know what the refrigerator costs?

JULIE: I haven't committed to the Gaggenau yet.

MAGGIE: Can you play hooky today? We need to look at some cabinets.

JULIE: We settled on the Thermofoil.

MAGGIE: They screwed up. Three weeks delivery turned into three months.

JULIE: Oh god . . .

MAGGIE: But—I found a cancelled order, in stock, seriously worth a look . . .

JULIE: Ohhh . . . I am reaaaally behind at work.

MAGGIE: They're *not* Thermofoil. They're reaaaally nice; you'll save a fortune . . .

JULIE: Meet you at one?

MAGGIE: Brilliant. And you saw the link I sent you?

JULIE: "Madagascar"?

MAGGIE: What do you think?

MAGGIE holds up her iPad to show JULIE the page.

JULIE: *(quietly, longingly)* It's beautiful, it's stunning, but how could we possibly fit a kitchen island?

MAGGIE: Like . . . this.

MAGGIE swipes on the iPad. JULIE gasps. Stares. Looks at the wall that divides the kitchen from the dining room. Back at the iPad.

JULIE: Knock it down?

MAGGIE: Uh-huh.

JULIE snaps back to reality.

JULIE: Don't ever show me that again.

MAGGIE: Really no?

JULIE: *Really* no.

JULIE gets her stuff ready for work.

And I really have to get to work so I can sneak out to meet you.

WAYNE *enters followed by* JOHN.

WAYNE: Okay, it's not such a big deal, it's all fixable.

JULIE: What's fixable?

WAYNE: While we were taking out the old plaster, a few bricks fell out of the wall.

JOHN: Just the places Wayne was hitting really hard with the sledgehammer.

JULIE: You hit our wall with a sledgehammer?

JOHN: And a bunch of bricks popped out of the outside layer of the wall. They're lying in your garden, but I found most of them.

JULIE: In my *garden*?

WAYNE: Calm down, I will fix it.

JULIE: Do you know how to do that?

WAYNE: I will research it.

JULIE: Let's just call a professional.

WAYNE: And blow the contingency fund? I will not be doing that.

JULIE: John, would your father know how to fix it?

JOHN: Oh, definitely.

WAYNE: Every time we call John's father he charges me two hundred dollars.

JOHN: Only the times he's had to come over.

JULIE: John, call your father, let's get one thing done right—

WAYNE: Don't touch that phone! I will research how to fix the bricks and then John and I will fix the bricks. We were going to be fixing bricks anyway when we move the window.

JOHN: I don't know anything about working with bricks.

WAYNE: What? Moving the window is in the design book!

JOHN: That's masonry work, you have to call someone in.

WAYNE: Is that costed in?

JOHN: Nothing's costed in. You decided to pay me by the hour.

JULIE: Wayne, just call his dad—

WAYNE: I am researching it tonight, we're fixing it tomorrow, and then we're moving the window and sending back the table saw.

JULIE: The what?

JOHN: You bought a table saw?

WAYNE: It's a DeWalt.

JOHN: Sweeeeet!

JULIE: You bought a *table saw*?

WAYNE: I got excited and bought something totally necessary, but I've seen the light. I'm sending back the DeWalt—

JULIE: Wayne, slow down—

WAYNE: —and we're sending back the carafe and the recycler and all the K-Cups—

JULIE: Wayne, stop—

WAYNE: —and I'm going to fix the wall so we can stay on budget and on schedule!

JULIE: —take a walk and breathe—

WAYNE: No, just give me the sledgehammer; I want to find something to break!

JULIE: John, go to the kitchen. Maggie, go buy something.

> JOHN *and* MAGGIE *back away from the angry man.* MAGGIE *heads for the front.* JOHN *reaches the edge of the drop cloth and freezes, then turns and runs the other way.* MAGGIE *exits.* WAYNE *with his sledgehammer fixes his eyes on the Keurig machine.*

Wayne!

He comes back to Earth.

WAYNE: Sorry. A little out of control.

JULIE: We just had a little setback. There's going to be setbacks, we're okay with that. We're going to get there. We're going to have a kitchen.

WAYNE: Okay.

WAYNE *starts heading towards the basement stairs.*

JULIE: Where are you going?

WAYNE: Basement. I'll be fine.

WAYNE *exits downstairs.*

JULIE: Wayne?

JULIE is startled by a scream of rage from the basement. She shakes it off, grabs her coat for work, and exits the front door, where she passes JOHN *and* MAGGIE, *arms wrapped around each other.*

MAGGIE: What if we're married and we suddenly both get dream job offers in our dream cities but they're different cities?

JOHN: We figure it out.

MAGGIE: What if we're married but then there's a gender apocalypse, ninety percent of all the men are killed off, and you suddenly have your pick of the hottest babes on the planet?

JOHN: I already do.

MAGGIE: What if we're married and one of us decides to go vegan? What if we suddenly like different music? What if I decide I can't stand your friends? What if we end up becoming completely different people than we thought we were?

JOHN: What's going on?

MAGGIE: I don't think you've really been thinking this through.

JOHN: I'm good.

MAGGIE: What if we don't take the corner lot?

JOHN: Where would we put our little house?

MAGGIE: We could take all the money from this job and just travel until we run out and then take another job and do it again and again and again.

JOHN: As long as we're together, I love it. Just let me know by next Friday.

MAGGIE: Thinking.

They kiss. He exits to the house. She watches him. Frowns. Exits.

SCENE THREE

The plastic curtain is gone from the doorway and the walls are gutted to the studs, including both sides of the kitchen/dining room wall so that we can see the bare bones of what will hold the new kitchen. Squirming up the studs all around the kitchen are the new electrical cables. They run at odd angles through drilled holes in the wall with little apparent logic, eventually threaded into electrical boxes placed at seemingly random heights, many of them askew. It might look a bit like a child's drawing on an Etch A Sketch.

JOHN, holding the wiring diagram, stares at it all, baffled. WAYNE and JULIE beam proudly.

JOHN: Wow.

WAYNE: Eh?

JOHN: You did all this wiring yourself?

WAYNE: I worked in the basement, Julie pulled up the cables.

JULIE: Not bad for old folks, right?

WAYNE: Worked right through Sunday.

JOHN: I woulda come in if I'd known.

WAYNE: Three in the morning, but it's done.

JOHN: Amazing.

JULIE: Thank you, John. We are feeling mighty proud.

JULIE exits upstairs.

WAYNE: And we can move on to plumbing.

JOHN: Uh, Wayne?

WAYNE: Yo.

JOHN: What's this twenty-amp circuit for?

WAYNE: That's for . . . well, it must be for the microwave.

JOHN: *(off the diagram)* Nooo . . . the microwave's on the other wall.

WAYNE: Then it's for the garburator.

JOHN: The garburator gets a fifteen-amp circuit. And it goes on the other wall too, with the sink.

WAYNE: Then it's gotta be the microwave.

WAYNE stares at the wiring diagram, turns it around.

You got it backwards, genius. *(indicating north wall)* Sink here, garburator here, *(south wall)* microwave there.

JOHN: No, that's the north wall—

WAYNE: That's the *south* wall. Your sweetheart screwed up the directions in the drawing.

JOHN: That's the *north* wall where the window is.

WAYNE: That's the *south* wall, and your sweetheart put the window on the wrong side.

JOHN: And both the doors in the wrong place too?

Beat.

WAYNE: Crrrrrap.

JOHN: Rip them out?

WAYNE: No eff'n way. We're four days behind. Throw in some junction boxes, send a couple cables out to the other wall, we'll be done by afternoon.

JOHN: Two of the outlets are behind where the pantry goes, the stove's on the wrong side of the room—

WAYNE: John! Stop. We're not remeasuring and cutting and drilling everything all over again. We're just not.

JOHN: Honest, Wayne, every single box is in the wrong place. I don't even know how you could keep track of it all.

WAYNE: John, I'm handing you solutions, you're throwing back problems.

JOHN: It looks like it was done by a five-year-old.

WAYNE: It'll be covered with drywall, who cares?

JOHN: The inspector.

WAYNE: No permit, no inspector.

JOHN: No permit?

WAYNE: No sane person I know would ever pay the city for a permit allowing him to renovate his own house.

JOHN: There will be an inspector.

WAYNE: There won't be an inspector.

JOHN: My dad is an inspector.

Pause.

WAYNE: You could have told me that.

JOHN: I probably should have mentioned it, yes.

WAYNE: Before you had me invite him in to see the kitchen we were about to renovate.

JOHN: Get started?

WAYNE: I need a minute.

WAYNE exits to the basement. JOHN fits in some earplugs and starts unthreading cable ends from the electrical boxes. Nothing's been stapled yet. JULIE enters.

JULIE: Maggie coming?

He pulls the plugs out.

JOHN: Sorry?

JULIE: I said—

She's interrupted by the screams from WAYNE in the basement. JOHN reinserts the plugs. JULIE waits it out. MAGGIE enters, carrying her bag and holding her ears. JOHN and MAGGIE exchange a kiss, ears still held. The scream ends.

JOHN pulls the plugs out again.

JOHN: All clear.

JOHN heads down the basement stairs.

MAGGIE: Decision day!

JULIE: Homework done, I'm ready.

MAGGIE: One? Or two?

JULIE: It's two.

MAGGIE: I'm so happy for you!

JULIE: No, you're right, it's all about the resale value.

MAGGIE: Oh, when you're building at this level, in this neighbour-hood? If you don't have steam *and* convection ovens, you're just throwing away money.

JULIE: But I'm cutting corners and going with AEG for both. And I just can't buy a Gaggenau fridge—

MAGGIE: I hear you.

JULIE: I'm settling for the Liebherr.

MAGGIE: With a package deal you probably just saved yourself about five thousand.

JULIE: I know. Not that it'll make you-know-who any happier.

MAGGIE: Wait'll he sees it. Are you thinking cooktops?

JULIE: Night and day. I want a Bosch!

MAGGIE: Niiiice! But.

JULIE: What?

MAGGIE: We have to lose something.

JULIE: What do you mean?

MAGGIE: A pair of lower cabinets or a set of drawers?

JULIE: Why?

MAGGIE: With the bigger fridge, the two ovens, we can't fit your dishwasher.

JULIE: Oh no . . .

MAGGIE: Unless . . . Have you looked at the link I sent this morning?

JULIE: *(slightly pained)* The Galapagos? No.

MAGGIE takes out her iPad.

MAGGIE: Julie, if you take this step, you can have everything. You won't be shaping your house anymore, your house will start shaping you.

JULIE: NO.

MAGGIE: It's gone.

JULIE: And I've REALLY got to get to the office this afternoon.

MAGGIE: Then let's go get you some appliances.

They're startled by a sound. They turn around to see one of the cables has been pulled from below and is disappearing down into the floor like the carrots disappearing underground one after another from Elmer Fudd's garden.

JULIE: *What?*

And MAGGIE gets an email alert.

MAGGIE: *(off her phone screen)* What? *What?*

MAGGIE scrolls through a message while JULIE watches another cable struggle loose from its moorings and vanish.

JULIE: *(calling)* Wayne!

Another. This time JULIE runs for it. If she gets it, she'll wrestle the serpent. If not, she'll go for the next one.

MAGGIE: *(calling while still reading)* Johhhn?

JULIE: Wayne, stop it!

WAYNE: *(from below)* Julie, what the hell are you doing?

JULIE: What the hell are *you* doing?

MAGGIE: JOHN!

JOHN: *(from below)* What?

WAYNE: *(from below)* Julie, let go!

JULIE: You made me work on that for fourteen hours!

MAGGIE: Get up here right now!

JULIE: *(to MAGGIE)* *What?*

JULIE of course releases the wire, which is followed by big crashing sounds below.

JOHN arrives, having run up the stairs.

JOHN: 'Kay 'kay 'kay! What?

MAGGIE: Check your email!

JOHN: Why?

MAGGIE: Give me that.

MAGGIE grabs his phone, checks it.

JOHN: What are you looking for?

MAGGIE: No. Oh crap.

JOHN: What?

MAGGIE is still working his phone.

MAGGIE: Checking the website.

JOHN: Mags, *what?*

MAGGIE points to her phone. JULIE is now edging closer.

As JOHN reads off MAGGIE's phone, WAYNE emerges from the basement, very unhappy.

WAYNE: *(menacingly)* Julie . . .

JULIE: *Shht!*

JOHN: *(shocked)* Mags . . .

MAGGIE: Yeah.

JOHN: You made the cut . . .

MAGGIE: Yeah . . . I frikkin' did.

WAYNE: She what?

JULIE: Please spill. Please?

JOHN: Mars 100. Maggie's in.

JULIE: In what?

JOHN: Mars 100? Are you kidding? Mars 100? You don't know about Mars 100? To Mars?

WAYNE: Mars wasn't invented when we were kids.

JOHN: One hundred people are going to Mars. Maggie just made the shortlist for the first crew of *four*.

WAYNE: Maggie? *This* Maggie?

JOHN: Celebrity. Maggie. Superstar. Here.

MAGGIE: I'm going to Mars.

JULIE: With—what? NASA?

MAGGIE & JOHN: *(snort laughing)* NASA!

JOHN: NASA's about a century behind. This is the Mars 100 mission.

WAYNE: We got that part, keep going.

JOHN: Two hundred thousand people applied for this worldwide.

JULIE: And this Maggie made the shortlist?

JOHN: Yes!

JULIE: Maggie, how are you qualified to do that?

MAGGIE: I am highly skilled, I have a physics degree with an astronomy minor, and I sent a really good video.

WAYNE: Wait wait wait. Who is running this?

JOHN: A bunch of dudes in Europe.

JULIE: Dudes who own a rocket?

JOHN: Not yet, obviously.

WAYNE: But they will by . . . ?

JOHN: 2029. Ten years to get ready.

JULIE: To fly to Mars and back?

MAGGIE: Not back. It's a one-way trip.

WAYNE: Not back?

JOHN: You're missing the whole point.

MAGGIE: We're going there to live. We're going to colonize Mars.

WAYNE: Four people? To populate a planet?

JULIE: How many children are you planning to *have*?

JOHN: No, jeez! There's going to be a hundred. You aren't listening!

JULIE starts checking this on her phone.

MAGGIE: Every two years another crew joins us until there's a reasonable sized society. And then babies, maybe. But I might be as old as you guys by then, so—

WAYNE: *How* is this going to be paid for?

JOHN: It's going to be the first reality show from space—it's brilliant!

WAYNE: A reality show.

JOHN: Just look it up!

JULIE: *(off her phone)* Is this it? "Is Mars 100 a Hoax?"

JOHN: No, forget that garbage!

MAGGIE: That is the number one thing I hate about the Internet!

JOHN: Mags, get away from them.

JOHN guides MAGGIE over to a comfy chair.

You okay?

MAGGIE: Sorry, spinning here.

JULIE: *(off her screen)* "From the first shortlist of one thousand candidates, four will eventually be chosen. They are to live together in a small spaceship for the year-long flight to the red planet, where they will start building their home on Mars."

(quietly, to WAYNE) That doesn't really sound possible, does it?

WAYNE: Uh, no.

MAGGIE: John . . . You're not on the list.

JOHN: My email's sometimes wonky. Could still be coming.

MAGGIE: All the names are on the site.

JOHN: Oh. Crap.

MAGGIE: Yeah.

JOHN: I guess I'm phoning the bank to cancel.

MAGGIE: No, we're talking. Eyes. Give me eyes.

They lock eyes.

WAYNE: Okay, I'm going to finish—

JULIE motions him to shut up.

MAGGIE: What do I do?

JOHN: Come on. You know.

MAGGIE: No, I don't. What do I do?

JOHN: You go to Mars.

MAGGIE: You sure?

JOHN: I would.

MAGGIE: No, you wouldn't.

JOHN: Totally would.

MAGGIE: *With* me, you would.

JOHN: *(admitting it)* Yeah.

MAGGIE: This might actually happen.

JOHN: I so know that.

> WAYNE *and* JULIE *exchange a look of disbelief but keep listening.*

MAGGIE: It really could happen. John, I really really want this.

JOHN: You're clear I'm clear on that, right?

MAGGIE: We can't build our house.

JOHN: Of course we can. We still have ten years together.

MAGGIE: And get married?

JOHN: Duh.

MAGGIE: Even if?

JOHN: I am so in, no matter what.

MAGGIE: No matter what?

JOHN: No matter what.

WAYNE and JULIE are now gape-mouthed.

MAGGIE: I might have to move to Europe for training.

JOHN: Love Europe.

MAGGIE: Or suddenly move into isolation to test our psychological fortitude for like eight years.

JOHN: Mags. The less time we have together, the more I want to spend every minute of it with you.

MAGGIE moves closer.

MAGGIE: Really gotta think, okay? A lot.

JOHN: Still got five days. Wanna think together?

MAGGIE: Yeah.

JOHN and MAGGIE begin to walk out hanging on to each other, forgetting MAGGIE's bag on the table. They open the front door to the sound of showering rain. They look dreamily into each other's eyes, pull their jackets over their heads, and exit attached in a snuggle. WAYNE and JULIE are still staring.

JULIE: Mars? This can't be for real. Can it?

WAYNE: No way is it for real.

JULIE: We have to talk to them.

WAYNE: Don't even try it.

JULIE: We have to talk some sense into them.

WAYNE: How many times did you try to talk sense into our own kids?

JULIE: Yeah.

WAYNE: Not our problem. Our problem is that this kitchen will either save us, or kill us.

JULIE: What do you need me to do?

WAYNE: The same thing we did for fourteen hours yesterday.

JULIE nods grimly, grabs a demo suit, and they head for the basement. WAYNE returns for the wiring diagram. Orients it properly. Heads towards the basement. Sees something out the window.

Julie? There's a truck outside unloading something.

JULIE: *(from downstairs)* In this rain?

WAYNE: I think it's our cabinets!

WAYNE and JULIE scream. They run out the front door to the boom of a prairie downpour.

SCENE FOUR

The kitchen and everywhere else is now filled with large, wet cartons.

WAYNE and JULIE slump into chairs, exhausted and a little wet from the receiving emergency. WAYNE pulls out a utility knife, slices the tape on one of the cardboard boxes.

JULIE: What are you doing?

WAYNE: I want to make sure they're okay.

JULIE: Just before you open that—

But he's tearing it open, a bit like Christmas.

WAYNE: And I want to see if they're as beautiful as I think they are.

JULIE: You need to know there was a problem with the order—

He pulls out a cabinet. It's high-end solid wood.

WAYNE: Oh crap. Are they all like this?

JULIE: I think they probably are.

WAYNE: You think they got the whole order wrong?

JULIE: They were completely out of our choice.

WAYNE: Out of Thermofoil? Every place we've been to carries Thermofoil.

JULIE: We had a second thought about the Thermofoil.

WAYNE: What are you talking about?

JULIE: The order was going to be three months late, so when we went to reorder from another company we started thinking again—

WAYNE: I don't remember being consulted on this.

JULIE: End of the line, they had everything we needed, we saved a ton—

WAYNE: This is maple. You bought maple?

JULIE: *This* is a game changer.

WAYNE: How much?

JULIE: What you have to keep in mind is that house values in this neighbourhood are as high as they are because of the uniform quality of the houses.

WAYNE: Price?

JULIE: And if you want to achieve that level of value, you have to build to that level of quality.

WAYNE: Price?

JULIE: If we put in cheap cabinets, we might as well just burn the money we're spending on the polished stone floors and quartz countertops.

WAYNE: Price price price price price price price price—

JULIE: Seventeen thousand dollars!

WAYNE: We were going to pay eight! You doubled it! You more than doubled it!

JULIE: You promised not to dick around about prices!

WAYNE: You promised not to do what you're doing!

JULIE: They are twenty-five percent off. We're saving money!

WAYNE: VETO!

JULIE: For something beautiful instead of an ugly pile of crap!

WAYNE: VETO!

JULIE: We saw the best deal in the world and we grabbed it!

WAYNE: This is what you do! We discuss, we have thoughtful deep discussions, you make agreements, you turn around and do whatever the hell you want to!

Their fight continues as JULIE *retreats to another part of the house,* WAYNE *following, just as* JOHN *and* MAGGIE *enter through the front door.*

JOHN: *(simultaneously)* Name of moons?

JULIE: *(simultaneously offstage)* Oh my god, relax! We built in a contingency fund, okay?

MAGGIE: *(simultaneously)* Phobos and Deimos.

WAYNE: *(simultaneously offstage)* Three grand! That's our ten percent contingency!

JOHN: *(simultaneously)* Equatorial diameter?

JULIE: *(simultaneously)* Twenty percent, Wayne!

MAGGIE: 6,805 kilometres.

JOHN: Length of day?

MAGGIE: Twenty-four hours, thirty-seven minutes, and twenty-two seconds.

> *MAGGIE grabs the bag she forgot as JULIE and WAYNE return, their argument still going.*

WAYNE: Ten? Twenty? Who cares? You don't! You've spent the contingency and you couldn't care less!

> *MAGGIE and JOHN head back out the front door.*

JOHN: Length of year?

MAGGIE: 686.98 Earth days.

WAYNE: Hey, Buck Rogers! Barbarella! Get back here!

JOHN: Coffee.

JULIE: Use the Keurig! That's why I bought it!

JOHN: Surface temperature?

MAGGIE: Minus eighty-seven to minus five.

JOHN and MAGGIE *exit.*

WAYNE: And they're gone again.

JULIE: Wayne?

WAYNE: Is this a conspiracy? Are you all planning my death?

JULIE: Wayne.

WAYNE: What?

She shows him her phone.

What is that?

JULIE: Maggie's been showing me kitchen islands. This one is code-named Santorini.

WAYNE: You're not seriously thinking . . . ?

JULIE: I want it. So badly.

WAYNE: Julie, god sakes, you would have to tear down that whole wall. *No!*

JULIE: I already decided that. I didn't even ask you. I just said no. I just wanted you to know I did that.

WAYNE: It's pretty.

JULIE: It's stunning.

WAYNE: Yeah. It really is.

JULIE: Well, that wouldn't be just a kitchen. It would transform the whole house.

WAYNE: How much?

JULIE: Fifteen thousand . . .

She does the "more or less" gesture.

WAYNE *looks at the phone, rubbing his stomach.*

WAYNE: It's really nice . . .

JULIE: Completely impossible. Isn't it?

WAYNE: You could argue we might get it back on the sale.

JULIE: If we do it well we'd get it more than back.

WAYNE: I get what you're saying about the level of quality . . . that's not just a kitchen.

JULIE: Oh, with this kind of transformation, it's not us shaping the house anymore, the house starts shaping us.

WAYNE: It's a really bad idea.

JULIE: It'd be crazy.

WAYNE *rubs his stomach.*

WAYNE: Yeah.

JULIE: I want it . . .

WAYNE: I do too.

They hold hands. JULIE dials. WAYNE breathes deeply and massages his developing ulcer.

JULIE: *(on phone)* Ground control to Major Tom. Return to planet please, we are go on Santorini.

They exit.

SCENE FIVE

All of the spaghetti wiring has been removed from the kitchen/dining room stud wall. The kitchen is strung with work lights and extension cords. WAYNE and JOHN carry in a second, nearly identical, cripple wall—a temporary support frame of two-by-fours to hold the ceiling up until the new beam is in place for the open concept kitchen and dining room of their dreams. They fit it between ceiling and floor and screw it in place.

WAYNE: That'll hold, don't you think?

JOHN: I'd feel a whole lot better about this if we got my dad over here.

WAYNE: It ain't rocket science, buddy.

JOHN: What's that supposed to mean?

WAYNE: Relax, young Skywalker. It means *This Old House* says this is how you do it. *Holmes on Homes* says this is how you do it. Five other YouTubes say this is how you do it. We're doing it.

WAYNE picks up a reciprocating saw.

JOHN: Your call.

JOHN takes out his phone.

WAYNE: Hey! Could use some help here?

JOHN: Texting Maggie.

WAYNE: I'm cutting!

JOHN: It's not my idea.

WAYNE: Let Princess Leia wait two minutes and help me. I'm not kidding!

JOHN: I'm not going anywhere near that.

As JOHN texts tensely, JULIE enters tensely, headed for the door. She sees WAYNE cutting through the first stud. She stares in fear.

JULIE: *(over the saw)* WAYNE, WHAT ARE YOU DOING?

WAYNE: QUIET!

JULIE: SHOULDN'T JOHN BE USING THE SAW?

WAYNE pulls out the dangling half stud with authority, points to the door.

WAYNE: You—out.

She inhales deeply and passes JOHN, who is putting away his phone and pulling out a cigarette. WAYNE,

JULIE, *and* JOHN *all have identical expressions of intense preoccupation.*

JULIE: Morning, John.

JOHN: Maggie call you?

JULIE: Nope. You don't smoke.

JOHN: I know.

JOHN *heads for the back door,* JULIE *for the front door, and nearly smashes into* MAGGIE *entering with her bag and enormous travel mug.*

MAGGIE: You said you were taking the day off.

JULIE: Gotta show my face at work or I'm in it deep.

MAGGIE: Talk?

JULIE: Fast.

JOHN *returns at the sound of* MAGGIE's *voice, hiding the cigarette.*

JOHN: Mags!

MAGGIE *sees* WAYNE *cutting studs.*

MAGGIE: HO-LEE CRAP.

JULIE: *(over the saw, to* MAGGIE*)* WHAT?

JOHN: *(over the saw)* ELEVEN FORTY-FOUR.

MAGGIE: *(over the saw)* I'M ON IT.

JOHN: *(over the saw)* 'KAY, BUT, MAGS?

MAGGIE: *(over the saw)* I'M ON IT.

JOHN: *(over the saw)* YOU KNOW WHAT TIME IT IS, RIGHT?

MAGGIE: *(just as the saw stops, erupting)* YES, I KNOW WHAT FRICKING TIME IT IS!

> *Caught completely off guard,* JOHN *exits, slipping the cigarette back in his mouth.*

(to JULIE*)* Countertop's being held. Stick down a deposit.

JULIE: Got it—

MAGGIE: The cabinets broke my card. I can't keep floating this, we need a payment *now.*

JULIE: You're right, I'll get you the whole amount today. Anything else?

> MAGGIE *stares at her a moment, contemplating sharing something.*

What?

MAGGIE: Nothing.

JULIE: *(stopping her)* What?

MAGGIE: I'm not that trusting. Mother issues.

JULIE: Me neither. Daughter issues. Tell me.

WAYNE starts on the next stud. A sputtering and sparking of electricity from one of the exposed wires. The saw stops, all the work lights go out.

WAYNE: Crap!

JULIE: *(deflating)* Oh lord help me.

WAYNE heads for the basement.

MAGGIE: Where'd John go?

JULIE: What's going on? Just tell me.

MAGGIE: Lots.

JULIE: Yes . . . ?

MAGGIE: Time. I have twelve minutes left to make a decision.

JULIE: Maggie, is it about this ridiculous Mars thing, because if it is—

MAGGIE: Way too much sharing. Clock's ticking.

JULIE: What happens in twelve minutes?

JOHN re-enters through the back door. Timidly. The kitchen work lights snap back on, coincidentally perhaps illuminating JOHN.

JOHN: Hey, Maggie.

MAGGIE: Sorry.

WAYNE returns from the basement. Across the room JULIE signals him to shut up.

Way too caffeinated. Running about twelve scenarios in my head right now.

JOHN: You . . . thinking anything I should hear about?

MAGGIE: Eyes. John?

MAGGIE's body language is becoming squirmy.

JOHN: Gotta pee?

MAGGIE: Really bad.

JOHN: Want me to carry you?

MAGGIE: You know anything can change, right? ANYTHING! ANYTIME!

JOHN: Yeah. S'okay.

MAGGIE: If this is going to happen it's 'cause we make it happen and we're not giving it up for anything, no matter what.

JOHN: I'm with you.

MAGGIE: 'Kay.

JOHN: 'Kay we keep the land, 'kay we build the house, or 'kay we get married?

MAGGIE: Need three minutes.

JOHN shows her his phone.

JOHN: Real quick, our whole twenty-five thou goes non-refundable in nine.

MAGGIE: Right back.

MAGGIE grabs her purse, sees JULIE staring, and whips a finger towards her.

Countertops. Us. Money.

JULIE: Aye aye.

MAGGIE exits to the bathroom and JULIE works her phone screen. JOHN stands immobile.

WAYNE: Land, house, and marriage?

JOHN: Yeah. Maybe. Might not be though. Hard to say. Let you know in three minutes.

WAYNE: No hurry.

JOHN: How many scenarios do you run in your head?

WAYNE: You're a guy. If we could do what they can do, we'd be girls. Or a different species. Same thing, really.

JOHN: No. She's just really really goddamn amazing.

JULIE: *(off her phone screen)* Wayne?

WAYNE: Right here, love of my life.

JULIE: Is there a reason I can't make a payment with the Visa?

WAYNE: Did you go over the limit?

JULIE: We got our limit raised last month. Unless you didn't pay it?

WAYNE: Okay, yes, that's another possible explanation.

JULIE: *(another discovery)* Wayne, why is our bank account overdrawn?

WAYNE: It isn't overdrawn, I moved twenty thousand into it when we started ripping out the cupboards.

JOHN: Twenty *thousand?*

JULIE: *(still at her phone screen)* Oh, damn you. The line of credit too?

WAYNE: Where do you think I got the twenty thousand?

JOHN: If you've got twenty thousand, why are we paying for everything?

WAYNE: So we can afford to help you kids out.

JOHN: How are you helping us?

WAYNE: By giving you all this work.

JOHN: Great, could you help us out by paying us?

WAYNE: John, a deal is a deal.

JULIE: What happened to our tax-free savings account?

WAYNE: Would you stop panicking? We are not overdrawn.

JULIE shows him her phone.

JULIE: We are overdrawn! The numbers are all red!

WAYNE takes her phone.

WAYNE: What the hell did you do?

JULIE: What the hell did *you* do? This is supposed to be your job!

WAYNE: What's this three thousand dollars?

JULIE: That's the flooring. I told you all about that—

WAYNE: You weren't supposed to pay for that! *They're* supposed to pay for that!

JULIE: Wayne, they don't have any money. I paid them back!

WAYNE: We're supposed to pay for it when we can afford it, in six months.

JOHN: *Six months?*

WAYNE: Or whenever, don't worry about it.

JULIE: Wayne, we have money! Where is it?

WAYNE: *I* don't know! I'm looking! What are all these automatic withdrawals?

JULIE: We do everything on automatic withdrawals, you know that!

WAYNE: Do we? I don't know that!

JULIE: How can you not know that? They show up in the account every month!

JOHN: We aren't waiting six months to get paid!

JULIE: I asked you to do the laundry and the books. That's it. Your only two jobs and you can't do either of them?

WAYNE: Don't start on the laundry. We both know I shouldn't be in charge of laundry!

JOHN: One of you tell me we're going to get paid!

JULIE: Just give it a second, John, until we figure out why we're bankrupt.

JOHN: *Bankrupt?*

WAYNE: Look at all these Starbucks! How many lattes do you drink in a day?

JULIE: I did not drink twenty thousand dollars in lattes.

WAYNE: What appliance costs *eight thousand dollars?*

JULIE: Our refrigerator, obviously.

WAYNE: Is this nine thousand dollars for the oven?

JULIE: Of course not! It's two ovens.

WAYNE: *(still off the screen)* Oh my god!

JULIE: You approved it.

WAYNE: What did you buy for *twenty-eight thousand dollars?*

MAGGIE enters from the bathroom.

JOHN: What the hell?

JULIE: The government took it. That's my income tax!

WAYNE: It comes off your paycheque!

JULIE: You said we could make interest off the money! You said we should pay it in a lump sum!

WAYNE: Why didn't you tell me I said that?

JOHN: How can you not have any money?

WAYNE: *(blurting)* Because of all her lattes!

MAGGIE: Who doesn't have any money?

JOHN: They can't pay us, they're bankrupt!

JULIE: Wayne, it's way bigger than the lattes!

MAGGIE: *Bankrupt?*

WAYNE *tries to pull it back again.*

WAYNE: I know! I know it's not the lattes, but look at them all!

MAGGIE: We've got twenty thousand in materials we *fronted* you.

JULIE *notices the plastic stick in* MAGGIE's *hand.*

JULIE: Maggie, what is that?

MAGGIE: No, not twenty, to hell with that. Markup and labour included, thirty grand.

JULIE: Maggie, show me the stick.

MAGGIE: No, screw thirty. Make it fifty. Contract breeched, fraud, damages—*stress*!

MAGGIE *points to her stomach.*

Yes, stress! Danger to life!

JULIE: Oh no.

JOHN: Mags, what are you talking about?

MAGGIE: The whole enchilada. We are so suing their asses. I told you I hated these scumbags.

JOHN *takes out his phone.*

JOHN: Mags, focus, two minutes, gotta call it . . .

MAGGIE: No worries, the land's paid for now. We're taking their house and we're selling it.

WAYNE: You can't, it's mortgaged into the next century.

JOHN's phone is in hand.

JOHN: Mags, like one minute, calling or not calling?

MAGGIE: John? God! *(pointing)* Stick. Blue. Baby.

JOHN: *(totally news)* Baby?

JULIE: Yes, duh! Baby!

MAGGIE: Don't you duh him, baby boomer asshat!

JOHN: You and me?

JULIE: For god sakes, I know that blue stick too well, I have three grown daughters. I will drive you to the abortion clinic!

MAGGIE: That is so your generation! Abort! Abort!

JULIE: What? Are *you* pro-lifing me?

MAGGIE: Move over, bitch, time to let someone else drive!

JOHN: Mags, dialing? What do I do?

MAGGIE: *(to WAYNE)* House equity?

WAYNE makes a "tiny bit" gesture.

WAYNE: Like this?

MAGGIE: Oh, I hate you so much.

JOHN: Mags?

MAGGIE: *(to JOHN)* Baby?

JOHN: Love babies.

MAGGIE: Really really?

JOHN: Love 'em love 'em.

MAGGIE: Land, house, baby?

JOHN: I want them all.

MAGGIE: Me too. Let's get married.

JULIE: Idiots.

JOHN: No call?

MAGGIE: No call.

> JOHN *puts down the phone.*

JOHN: I love you.

MAGGIE: I love you too.

> MAGGIE *turns to* WAYNE.

And I fucking *hate* you.

WAYNE: I understand your heightened emotions. And yes, we're broke.

MAGGIE: People die from being hated as much as I hate you.

JULIE: I am dangerously close to agreeing.

MAGGIE: And you're on the same list.

WAYNE: Okay, look. This talk of hate is all very fun, but I think it's time to stop the blaming and realize we're all in this mess together.

JOHN: What "together"?

MAGGIE: Our next date's in court, asswipe.

WAYNE: Thank you for that update from the Martian bureau.

JOHN: One more of those, buddy—

JULIE: There is only one person to blame here, Wayne.

WAYNE: (*dangerous*) What?

JULIE: And I'm trying not to say who it is, but oh my god.

WAYNE: (*warning*) Julie—

JULIE: How is it possible that a smart man like you can't add up a simple line of numbers so we can keep our home together?

WAYNE: How is it possible that a smart woman like you can't comprehend that we no longer have a two-income bank account? "Let's go to Mexico, let's go to Europe, let's buy a time-share. I'm tired of this car, I'm tired of these clothes, I'm tired of this furniture. Let's eat out and out and out, and I know, LET'S BUILD A NEW KITCHEN!"

JULIE: You are in charge of the money, not me! You are in charge of saying no!

WAYNE: No? No doesn't work on you! You are no proof! I've tried it in seventeen different languages, you don't speak any of them! How do you explain to a mad dog he should stop barking? How do you talk a lemming down off a cliff? I have this recurring nightmare. Iron Man is coming at me and I'm supposed to stop him from buying a ten thousand dollar fridge!

JULIE: Okay, Wayne, you're angry, let's talk about this later.

WAYNE: I'm sorry, did you want to run out and do some last minute shopping before the bank repossesses our house?

JULIE: Please, let's not talk about this in front of the kids—

WAYNE: Oh, it's the kids now, looks like we've adopted the little darlings. Lots of room, kids, come on in, sure hope you don't eat much!

JULIE: Wayne, stop it!

WAYNE: There's only one thing that scares me, Julie, and that's you. I am terrified of you. Because every plan we've come up with to save a penny for our old age, you have sabotaged them all. I don't know why you're trying to drive me to a heart attack, but the only possible explanation I can come up with is that you are either evil or stupid.

A long pause. MAGGIE and JOHN stare at JULIE. At WAYNE. At JULIE. JULIE exits upstairs.

JOHN: Dude.

MAGGIE: Dude.

JOHN: Not cool, Dude.

MAGGIE: Very very not cool.

WAYNE: She's had that coming a long time.

JOHN: Nope, don't think so.

MAGGIE: Major dick move.

JOHN: Even for you.

WAYNE: Normal marriage stuff. Get used to it. I'll sleep in the spare room, we'll make up in the morning. Or so.

> JULIE *comes down with a small packed suitcase, grabs her coat, and heads out the door.*

(calling after) Julie . . .

MAGGIE: That usually happen?

WAYNE: No.

JOHN: Wayne, dude, go after her.

WAYNE: I'm not going after her.

MAGGIE: Go!

> WAYNE *runs for it, opens the door. A car tears out of the driveway.*

WAYNE: *(from outside)* JULIE!

JOHN *closes the door.*

JOHN: And it's snowing.

MAGGIE: Old people. Promise we'll never be like them.

JOHN: Not in a million years. They can't really be broke.

MAGGIE: We'll figure it out tomorrow.

JOHN: We're having a baby. I love you. Forever.

MAGGIE: And I love you.

JOHN: And I'm sorry you're not going to Mars.

MAGGIE: I'm going to Mars, are you crazy?

JOHN: Hang on. We're getting the land?

MAGGIE: Yeah?

JOHN: And building a house, and getting married, and having a baby?

MAGGIE: Yeah?

JOHN: And if they call, you're still going?

MAGGIE: If I get called, I'm going. I said that. You knew that. Didn't you hear me say that? John? You're up to speed on this, right?

JOHN: Me, baby. You, Mars?

MAGGIE: I was clear. I was crystal perfect transparent spell-it-out clear. We were both perfectly clear. How could you not understand that?

The scales fall from JOHN's *eyes. He puts on a work coat.*

Where are you going?

JOHN: What the fuck, Maggie? What. The. Fuck?

MAGGIE: What? This is exactly what we just agreed to!

JOHN *heads out the door.*

What the hell?

MAGGIE *follows without a coat.*

John! Don't you drive off and leave me here!

There's suddenly the sound of sputtering and crackling. In the kitchen sparks are shooting out from an exposed electrical connection. The lights snap out.

End of Act One.

ACT TWO
SCENE ONE

A minute or two later. Darkness. The same wiring in the kitchen shoots sparks again. The lights snap back on. WAYNE re-enters from the front door.

WAYNE sighs in frustration.

A beat later, MAGGIE enters.

MAGGIE makes an identical sigh of frustration.

WAYNE: And it's snowing.

MAGGIE: Of course it is.

WAYNE: She's an idiot.

MAGGIE: She's not an idiot. You're an idiot and he's an idiot.

WAYNE: Why am I more of an idiot than she's an idiot?

MAGGIE: Because I was right here and I heard everything you said. You're the idiot.

WAYNE: It's called a fight. You'll be getting lots of practise.

MAGGIE: So what are you doing?

WAYNE: I told you. We're fighting.

MAGGIE: Your wife just drove off with her suitcase, why are you just standing here?

WAYNE: We sold the Saturn, she's got the SUV. What am I supposed to do?

MAGGIE: You've heard of a phone?

WAYNE: I'm not calling her.

MAGGIE: Why would you not?

WAYNE: She spent all our money, not me. She took off in the car, not me. She's the one who's wrong, not me.

MAGGIE: Oh my god! Get on the phone this second!

WAYNE: You don't call someone when you're both angry, you just end up screaming at each other.

MAGGIE: She's not going to scream at you. She's not even going to pick up!

WAYNE: Then why would I call her?

MAGGIE: So she knows you actually give a crap! How have you survived this long?

WAYNE: Maybe our generation just knows a thing or two about getting along, okay?

MAGGIE: Fine, it's your divorce.

Beat.

WAYNE: Okay, maybe one call.

WAYNE *picks up the land line.*

MAGGIE: Whoa whoa, what are you doing?

WAYNE: You said to call her.

MAGGIE: Whose name is that phone under?

WAYNE: Whose—what?

MAGGIE: Whose name will she see when her phone rings?

WAYNE: Hers, I guess.

MAGGIE: You're using her phone to call her on her phone. Does this sound like a mature adult calling his wife? Or a small child calling his mother?

WAYNE: You're overthinking this.

MAGGIE: This is modern communication. It cannot be overthought.

WAYNE: Then what am I supposed to do?

MAGGIE: Use your own phone.

WAYNE: This will be fine.

MAGGIE: You don't own a cellphone, do you.

WAYNE: Surviving fine without one.

MAGGIE: Oh my god.

WAYNE: I don't need a cellphone to have a fight with my wife!

MAGGIE: Walk through this. You call. She doesn't pick up. What do you do?

WAYNE: Leave a message?

MAGGIE: Exactly. And she listens to it when?

WAYNE: When she gets where she's going and stops driving.

MAGGIE: Did you see her leave? Did you listen to anything you said to her? She's not picking up anything from you for three days minimum!

WAYNE: Then why does it matter if I call her?

MAGGIE: How do you do this? How do you act like an asshole and still make me feel sorry for you? You're as pathetic as my dad but even older!

WAYNE: What? What am I doing that's so wrong?

MAGGIE: She's not going to listen to your message, so then what?

WAYNE: Then I wait.

MAGGIE: No. One is nothing. You have to show your pain.

WAYNE: I leave another one?

MAGGIE: Yes. And then?

WAYNE: Another one? I'm not the one who's wrong!

MAGGIE: And you're going to keep doing it. Six tightly spaced pleading voice mails before midnight. Six is the limit, midnight is the cut-off. And then you go to texting. Get to a mall this second and buy a phone.

WAYNE: If I've left six messages she hasn't listened to, why would I bother texting?

MAGGIE: Because a text is right on her phone, she can't help seeing it. You break right through her defences, full frontal assault.

WAYNE: Oh.

MAGGIE: And she's getting curious. She's been denying herself the satisfaction of listening to these voice mails all this time. But she figures it won't hurt if she peeks every now and then to see if you sound remorseful enough.

WAYNE: *(possibly getting it)* Right . . .

MAGGIE: One text and one only, twice a day, for forty-eight hours.

WAYNE: Why?

MAGGIE: Because texting is a precision tool for asking forgiveness. If you don't set a limit you'll overtext, you'll get sloppy, you'll start blaming or go passive-aggressive, then you'll be chain texting, you'll become pathetic, maudlin, and destructive.

WAYNE: Why should I trust any of this?

MAGGIE: Because I have a degree in conflict resolution.

AND—

She holds up her phone.

Because I grew up with these. Everything I've told you I learned the hard way.

Beat.

WAYNE: What if she hasn't answered after forty-eight hours?

MAGGIE: You send your first suicide threat.

WAYNE: Okay, enough. I know how to fight with my own wife.

WAYNE starts dialing.

MAGGIE: Fine fine fine fine fine fine fine fine fine!

MAGGIE grabs at the phone as WAYNE tries to protect it.

Use the land line, fine. But if she ever listens to this message, she will not go on to the next one unless this is sad and regretful and sincere. Forget this whole dickhead idea that she's wrong. You say three things and three only: "I am sorry. I was wrong. Please call me so we can talk about this." You hang up, wait two minutes, as if you're actually hoping she'll call back—which she won't—and then you call again.

WAYNE dismissively waves her off and dials.

MAGGIE starts leaving the room.

Good luck.

WAYNE: No, stay stay stay stay stay—

MAGGIE stays. WAYNE inhales for JULIE's greeting message.

Julie!

Checking with MAGGIE as he talks.

I am so so sorry.

A nod from MAGGIE.

I was wrong. I've never been so wrong before in my life.

Nod.

I love you. You are the moon and the stars to me . . .

MAGGIE indicates "more concise."

You are the path that I walk, the land I gaze upon—

MAGGIE indicates "get on with it."

Please, please, please forgive me?

MAGGIE gives a thumbs-up and the "call me" gesture.

Because, I mean, what am I supposed to do? I love you so much, but you can see my side of this, right?

MAGGIE gives him a danger signal, don't go there.

I mean, I know I get a share of this blame, but how can you not know this by now? This is obvious even to you, isn't it, honey? You know this is your fault. I could see that registering, and I'm sorry I yelled, I'm a yeller, you know that. I'm an Old Yeller. And you're another one. So I think you should just come home. I'll apologize to you, you'll apologize to me, and we're square. Okay, bye bye now.

WAYNE looks up with a smile. MAGGIE has long since ceased giving signals.

I think I know where I went off the rails there, I'll try again.

MAGGIE: Dude, you are so cut off voice mails. Just go straight to texting and good luck.

WAYNE: *(dialing)* Nope, I am doing this old school.

MAGGIE: You will fail miserably and die lonely if you do not switch to texting ASAP. Is your wife worth the cost of a cellphone?

Pause.

WAYNE: How much do they—

Pause. Off her look:

Right. Yes. Of course she is, thank you.

WAYNE goes for his coat. But stops.

Could you stay long enough to teach me how to text?

MAGGIE: I'm leaving the second John gets here. And then we're going back to suing your ass.

WAYNE: Right.

WAYNE gets his coat. But stops.

Why hasn't your phone been ringing this whole time?

MAGGIE: John won't call, he'll just come back.

WAYNE: Got ya.

WAYNE starts putting on his coat. But does one last Columbo.

And why is it you haven't been calling him?

MAGGIE: Because unlike your situation I really *am* not the one who is wrong.

WAYNE: You're right. He's probably on his way back here right now. He's probably even sorry about backing his truck out of my driveway so fast he took out my neighbour's tree. You know where the coffee is. See you in an hour.

MAGGIE: Why are you walking? Call a cab.

WAYNE: You believe you're going to Mars. You believe he's the one who's wrong. And you believe you can get a taxi in Winnipeg in a snowstorm.

WAYNE exits the front door with lots of winter clothes. MAGGIE takes out her cell. Glances at it. Does maybe a round or two of okay-I'll-call/no-not-calling. Then dials, puts the phone to her ear, and takes a big breath.

TIME SHIFT TO SCENE TWO

In a little mini movie of time passing, MAGGIE might silently pour some coffee, do some angry texting, peek out the window, second-think the wisdom of her text outburst, attempt some more reasonable texting, check the window, etc.

An hour or so later. MAGGIE on the most comfortable seat available in the clutter, is wrapped in a blanket, still texting madly—lots of rethinking, typing, deleting, retyping.

WAYNE enters the front door in the same winter clothes he left in. She looks up. He holds up the shiniest, newest, and biggest iPhone. Shocked, she mouths, "Holy shit!" He approaches without removing his winter clothes, hands her the phone, shrugging helplessly. She does a bunch of things with it indicating a super-speedy setup. Hands it back to him. He puts on reading glasses and pecks out a couple keys at Precambrian speed.

MAGGIE touches her phone and we hear the "whoosh" of her phone sending a message. Looks over at his phone. Rolls her eyes. Takes his phone. Types. Shows him. He nods, pleased. She touches the phone. Whoosh. Hands it back to him.

MAGGIE composes another. WAYNE thinks. Ponders. Thinks. Peeks over at her screen. Starts copying a letter at a time like he's cheating on an exam. She touches the phone. Whoosh. Holds her phone for him to copy off her screen. He touches the phone. Whoosh. She keeps texting. He keeps copying.

Lights fade, say halfway. MAGGIE drifts to sleep. WAYNE is still texting, copying off her phone, but gaining proficiency as he evolves to make use of his opposable thumbs. The "whoosh" sounds coming faster and faster, indicating a time-lapse. Until . . .

SCENE TWO

Same setting, continued action. The morning light fades up on WAYNE, now speaking as he texts.

WAYNE: " . . . so, so, so sorry. How could I even THINK such things. I ought to have my HEAD examined. As U R my Alpha, my Omega, I love u, I need u, I will die without u. What more can I say?"

He taps MAGGIE, holds the screen out for her. She opens one eye to check it.

MAGGIE: "How could I even think suck pigs?"

WAYNE: What? It doesn't say that.

MAGGIE scrolls up, reads another.

MAGGIE: "I ought to have head exactly?"

WAYNE: What the hell happened?

MAGGIE *finding another, laughing.*

MAGGIE: "You're a male that I am a guy I love you."

WAYNE: Oh god, are they all like that?

She scrolls, and they both see one too dirty to repeat.

MAGGIE: Maybe we'll turn off your autocorrect for now?

WAYNE: That took hours!

MAGGIE: Wait a minute. "Hashtag SoSoSorry." No.

WAYNE: What?

MAGGIE: "Hashtag WayneLovesJulie." Do NOT use hashtags for texting.

WAYNE: Everybody uses hashtags.

MAGGIE: And they're wrong, stop it right now.

WAYNE: Adds emphasis. "Hashtag WaitingUpAllNight."

MAGGIE: Then use emojis, not hashtags: Crying Face, Broken Heart, Smiley Poop.

WAYNE: Smiley Poop?

MAGGIE: I should be charging for this.

We hear a truck pulling up outside. WAYNE *runs for the window.*

WAYNE: Holy crap. It worked!

MAGGIE: He's here?

WAYNE: No! *She's* here!

MAGGIE: No frikkin' way.

We hear another truck.

WAYNE: Wait a minute. He's here too. What the hell?

MAGGIE: 'Bout time.

WAYNE: He's getting out. He's going back to talk to her. This is weird.

MAGGIE: What are they doing?

WAYNE: Talking.

MAGGIE: What about now?

WAYNE: Talking.

MAGGIE: What about now?

WAYNE grabs his coat.

What are you doing?

WAYNE heads for the door.

WAYNE: She's not coming in.

MAGGIE: Give her space.

WAYNE: You said I should throw myself on her mercy.

MAGGIE: That got her back to the house. Now go for respectful dignity.

WAYNE: Respectful dignity. Good plan.

As WAYNE puts his coat back, JOHN enters in full winter gear.

MAGGIE: Johnny?

JOHN: What are you doing here?

MAGGIE: Johnny, I'm sorry, I'm really really sorry. You know that by now, but you punished me really bad. You were really mean. I need sleep, can you take me home now, please?

JOHN: What are you talking about?

MAGGIE: Didn't you check my messages?

JOHN: What messages?

MAGGIE: I left you like a hundred voice mails and texts.

JOHN: I left my phone in the truck.

WAYNE: What's Julie doing out there?

JOHN: Nope.

WAYNE: What?

JOHN: You're not going out there.

WAYNE: Why not?

JOHN: Julie does not want to talk to you under any circumstances whatsoever.

WAYNE: *What?*

JOHN: She says she had to turn her phone off to sleep because you were annoying the crap out of her with a bunch of stupid texts.

WAYNE: Okay then.

> WAYNE *heads to the door.* JOHN *steps in his way.*

JOHN: I can't let you do that.

WAYNE: Get out of my way.

JOHN: You've hurt her very badly. Your behaviour was abominable, unacceptable, and a couple other things I can't remember, but I agree. So she asked me to meet her here so she doesn't have to step inside. She wants her Keurig machine.

WAYNE: I thought you left your phone in the truck.

JOHN: She emailed me.

WAYNE: Move.

JOHN: I don't want to hurt you.

WAYNE: I'm kind of in the mood to hurt someone, tough luck for you.

WAYNE takes a dukes-up fighting stance. JOHN matches it.

JOHN: You're going to hit me, Wayne?

WAYNE: If I have to.

JOHN: You're going to hit me, kick me, whatever it takes?

WAYNE: You got the picture.

JOHN: We're gonna wrestle and scream and roll around the floor and gouge each other's eyes out until someone's bleeding and yells uncle?

WAYNE: Let's go, tough guy!

JOHN shrugs and steps out of the way. WAYNE rushes out without a coat on.

MAGGIE: That's how you protect a woman?

JOHN: Her doors lock.

He picks up the coffee machine.

MAGGIE: That's it? You seriously came for the machine?

JOHN: Yup.

MAGGIE: John, I feel like crap, I need a ride home, please don't make me walk.

He puts the machine down by the door and pulls out his keys.

JOHN: Take it.

He drops the keys somewhere just out of her reach.

I'll use my dad's.

MAGGIE: Okay.

JOHN: You bet.

MAGGIE: A little tension here.

JOHN: Sure is.

MAGGIE: You seem angry.

JOHN: So do you.

MAGGIE: We have to talk about this.

JOHN: Should we pick up from, "Fuck you, you motherfucking selfish prick"?

MAGGIE: You *did* check your messages.

JOHN: One was enough.

MAGGIE: I think we can get past that now if we're both willing to listen.

JOHN: Go right ahead.

MAGGIE: We have to name the elephant in the room.

JOHN: Go for it.

MAGGIE: Is it the embryo?

JOHN: Is that what we're calling it?

MAGGIE: That's all it is. A little tiny clump of cells.

JOHN: Happy with the embryo.

MAGGIE: Getting married?

JOHN: Great with married.

MAGGIE: Mars?

He waits.

You just have to say it out loud. "I don't want you to go to Mars."

Pause.

Say it.

JOHN: I don't want you to go to Mars.

MAGGIE: Good. Good. There. That's how you feel?

JOHN: Yes.

MAGGIE: Then fuck you, you motherfucking selfish prick!

JOHN gets up to leave.

No! Wait! That's nothing!

He stops.

See? A little emotion and you run. What are you going to do when I start throwing punches?

He stares at her. Just then WAYNE enters through the front door wearing no coat and looking right ticked. They see him and stop talking. He gets his coat and boots and goes back out.

JOHN: *(resuming)* Now you want to punch me too?

MAGGIE: I'm not going to punch you, but we've never fought before. We have to learn to fight. I've never even seen you angry before.

JOHN: You've seen me angry lots of times.

MAGGIE: Yeah. When the Jets lose.

JOHN: Yeah, and other times. The Bombers.

MAGGIE: Okay, you're angry a lot, but not at *me*.

JOHN: Here's what's going to happen. We owe twenty-five grand to the municipality for a piece of land we aren't going to use and another twenty grand on ten different credit cards for the kitchen they don't want anymore. I went back to the municipal office, waited for two hours, argued for another half hour: they won't take the land back, it's an airtight deal. So we sell the land, I'll work every day until the damn kitchen is finished so they can sell the house and we can get at least some of our money back. And then if you decide to have the embryo, I will get whatever job I need to pay my half of the expenses until the embryo turns eighteen, whatever planet you raise her on.

MAGGIE: Johnny . . .

> WAYNE *enters, more ticked off still. They keep talking this time as he walks across the stage without removing his boots and exits the opposite side.*

JOHN: And if you don't keep the embryo, and if we come out of this with any profit, I'm taking my half and moving to China.

MAGGIE: You made a decision without me.

JOHN: I make lots of decisions without you.

> WAYNE *walks back across the stage with a coat hanger, untwisting the hook end as he goes.*

MAGGIE: You've never decided anything yourself. You let me decide absolutely everything. It's one of the things I can't stand about you.

> JOHN *picks up the Keurig.*

JOHN: Don't have to worry about that anymore.

MAGGIE: Okay, okay. I have a little obsession about Mars, and there's an embryo involved now, I get that. But it's okay, it's not a problem.

> JOHN *starts to exit.*

JOHN: Get out any drawings if you've got them, because when I get back I'll be putting in electrical boxes, and if you don't know where the light switches are going, then I'll decide that too.

MAGGIE: John, look! You shut up about this; you may never mention this again; this is a one-time event. Here.

She indicates an imaginary space.

Here is a box. Its walls are three feet thick. It's completely soundproof.

She pulls him inside the space.

We are inside the box now. I'm saying this once and only once and only inside this box. I'm not an idiot. I know the odds of Mars 100 ever *going* to Mars are about ten million to one. I know my odds of making the crew are even worse. Which means I'm also saying it's ten million to one that ten years from now I'll still be here on Earth. And that means, ten million to one, I'll be here, with you and our little nine-year-old embryo. And so Mars is not a problem, okay?

JOHN: That's what you believe?

MAGGIE: Silence. Step out of the box. Out.

She pushes him out and shrinks the box.

Shrinking it now. Dropping it in the ocean. Splash. Gone. We shall never speak of this again.

JOHN: Like hell we won't.

WAYNE re-enters through the front door, really mad now. He again crosses and exits the opposite side. JOHN continues overtop of WAYNE.

Playing it out as he speaks:

Bringing the box back up again. Step inside. You don't believe you're going to Mars?

MAGGIE: Aaaag! Yes I do. I totally believe it with every fibre of my being. Why don't you get this?

JOHN: Okay then. Old Maggie's back.

WAYNE recrosses, this time carrying a crowbar. Exits the front door.

MAGGIE: I want this. I've been obsessed with Mars since I was three years old. I want my life to be brave and huge and extraordinary, and this is biggest, hugest, most important thing I could ever dedicate my life to, and yes I would die on another planet because this one is screwed and the only chance for the long-term survival of our species is to leave Earth behind, and I did not say that, Stephen fucking Hawking said that, so if they call, yes I'm going.

JOHN: I know all this, Maggie.

MAGGIE: But privately, inside, obviously I get that this mission has no credibility, and I know there's almost no atmosphere on Mars. I wrote my thesis on the problem of radiation shielding and lack of replacement parts and food production and a thousand other problems. And even if it happens I realize that I would spend a very short and miserable and dusty life inside a tiny plastic box no bigger than this kitchen. It's impossible and ridiculous and everyone I know loves to point that out to me, but I still want to go. Do you see why I don't really like to say all this out loud?

JOHN: Because it's insane?

MAGGIE: Okay, look. Still inside the box?

JOHN: Yes.

MAGGIE: You say you want to get married.

JOHN: Yes.

MAGGIE: How can you do that?

JOHN: Get married?

MAGGIE: When you say you will love me for the rest of your life. Is that something you actually believe? Or is it just the thing you say because that's what people say?

JOHN: I know it.

> Around now JULIE enters, scowling and shaking her head in disbelief. She crosses the stage in the same route WAYNE's been making as JOHN and MAGGIE talk. They don't notice her.

MAGGIE: How can you know it? Do you mean you know it, like, this is one hundred percent the certifiable truth, I've been in a time machine, I've seen the future, and this truth is unshakable? Or do you mean I promise to love, honour, and respect you for the rest of our lives so help me god, but my fingers are crossed because we all know nobody stays married forever anymore?

JOHN: The first one. I just know it.

JULIE returns carrying a first aid kit. But this time she starts hearing the conversation as she passes.

MAGGIE: Then why am I the insane one? I have an insane wish, but I know it's insane. You have an insane wish, and you don't know it's insane. And bringing a baby into the world makes it even crazier. So why can't we both just have our insane wishes and pretend everything's fine the way everyone else does?

JULIE stops to watch. They're too absorbed to notice.

JOHN: Because me and the embryo can't be number two to Mars! You're making me feel like you just agreed to be my grad date, unless the school hockey star asks you later.

MAGGIE is about to jump in, but JOHN does her silence-with-a-raised-finger gesture.

Maggie. Forever.

WAYNE enters, clutching his hand, which may be dripping a little blood. JULIE signals him to be quiet and to listen.

Cross my heart. Stack of Bibles, so help me god. I had no idea I was a land and house and marriage and baby kind of guy. Until last night—suddenly I had them all at once. And I went, yup. That's me. That's what I want. And now I know. I can't be second choice. Me. Or Mars. Pick one.

MAGGIE: Land, house, marriage, baby. You won't give up any of them?

JOHN: Nope.

MAGGIE: But I'm supposed to give up my starving thin, one-chance-in-a-million dream to be by your side?

JOHN: But you want those same things!

MAGGIE: Who told you that?

JOHN: You did!

MAGGIE: Yes, I want them. But I want Mars too. And if you're asking me to give up Mars then you have to give up something.

JOHN: Can I give up smoking?

MAGGIE: Smoking?

JOHN: Never mind.

MAGGIE: Your choices are land, house, baby, marriage.

JOHN: House. No question.

MAGGIE: Too easy. We don't even have a house yet.

JOHN: Land. Putting it on Kijiji tomorrow.

MAGGIE: Mars is the biggest dream I've ever had. This has to hurt.

> *Pause.*

JOHN: I'm not giving up the embryo.

MAGGIE: Not your call.

JOHN: Nope. Your call. Totally your call. But if—whatever you decide—our little embryo makes it all the way to person-hood, then I want to be a part of it. I'm gonna be part of little Emmy's life.

MAGGIE: Okay. Totally reasonable. So that leaves . . . ?

JOHN: Marriage?

MAGGIE: Yeah?

JOHN: Who needs it? I give up on marriage.

MAGGIE: I don't believe you.

JOHN: There's only one reason I want you to marry me, Maggie. And that's because you love me as much as I love you and you want to spend the rest of our lives together. So I don't want to hear about marriage again until you've decided whatever you decide about houses and mortgages and little Emmy and Mars. And then we can figure it out.

MAGGIE: In three minutes we're stepping out of the box and lock-ing it and throwing it so far into the sea you will never find it again, understood?

JOHN: Got it.

MAGGIE: This is what scares me. When you say I love you, you always say forever. And it scares the hell out of me.

MAGGIE *takes his hands.*

I love you, John.

They kneel down face to face.

Right this moment. I'm with you.

JOHN: Good.

MAGGIE: But a year from now? How could I know? How can I promise you I'll love you forever? I don't know how I'm going to feel tomorrow.

JOHN: So life on Mars is no problem but life with me is too hard?

MAGGIE: We don't know anybody—anybody—who has even made it twenty years. None of our parents, none of our grandparents, nobody. And you just say, forever. Could we really do that?

JOHN: We do know two people, Mags.

MAGGIE: Who?

JOHN: Them.

MAGGIE: The walking dead?

JOHN: Yeah.

MAGGIE: That doesn't count.

JOHN: Thirty years. How did they do that?

MAGGIE: That's not love.

JOHN: Whatever it is, it's not impossible. If they can do it . . .

MAGGIE: That's not living.

JOHN: It may not be pretty, but if it's proof you want . . .

MAGGIE: That's not proof . . .

They suddenly jump and scream, both catching a glimpse of JULIE and WAYNE, who have been standing there outside the three-foot steel walls staring. MAGGIE and JOHN stand up slowly.

JOHN: Coffee?

MAGGIE: Yeah!

JOHN starts to exit.

JOHN: Good! Let's go get some!

MAGGIE stops at the doorway.

MAGGIE: In the snowstorm.

JOHN: The basement. For a moment.

MAGGIE: Yeah.

MAGGIE and JOHN exit to the basement.

WAYNE: Smug little pricks.

JULIE: God, we are getting old.

WAYNE: Wait'll they're our age. Then they'll be sorry.

JULIE: No, they're right. We disgust me too. We had what they had once. We could talk, we could communicate, we could work things out because we were the most important thing in the world to each other.

WAYNE: We can still do that.

JULIE: You keep saying we can: I don't see it. All I see is anger.

WAYNE: I'm not angry.

JULIE: You broke my car window with a crowbar. You dragged me into the house by force.

WAYNE: I did not use force.

JULIE: You suddenly thought you're a caveman. Whatever it is you've got to say, Grog, you better start grunting.

WAYNE: I'm working up to it.

JULIE: No working up. Last chance, Wayne. You saw how it's done. We're doing it just like them.

WAYNE: What are you talking about?

JULIE: Something about a box where you stand inside and be honest for once in your life. This is the marriage therapy you wouldn't do. If you've got something to be angry about, I want your honesty, your feelings. I want your guts. You've got two minutes.

WAYNE: Okay. Julie—

JULIE: And you can start by telling me, since when do you own a cellphone?

WAYNE: I just bought it. Last night.

JULIE: Like I'd believe that. Are you dealing?

WAYNE: What?

JULIE: I know what it means when your husband suddenly has a secret cellphone. I watched all five seasons of *Breaking Bad*.

WAYNE: I bought it so I could text my apologies to you!

JULIE: Why would you text when you can talk?

WAYNE: Because Maggie told me to!

JULIE: That's the stupidest thing I've ever heard. Have you got a lover?

> WAYNE *goes to take the new phone out of his back pocket.*

WAYNE: Julie, I got it six hours ago, it's brand new!

JULIE: Let me see this thing!

WAYNE: I'm trying! The stupid thing's too big!

> *He wrestles it out.*

There! Right out of the cellophane.

JULIE: You've got an iPhone X?

WAYNE: XS Max.

JULIE: Why am I stuck with an iPhone 6?

WAYNE: Maggie told me I had to text so you would see my apology. That's why I bought it, I swear to god!

JULIE: You spent money. You spent actual money.

WAYNE: Yes!

JULIE: Because that teenager told you to? Are you crushing on that girl?

WAYNE: Are you over crushing on your boyfriend with all his intact hair?

JULIE: Oh, get serious. I don't want hair and muscles and sexiness.

WAYNE: Oh good.

JULIE: You know what that boy has that I want? Forget the hair. Forget the vitality. I don't even care about the adoration he gives that girl. I want the commitment. I want the romance. She wants the stars, he flies off to get her one. I ask for the moon and you tell me it'll never fit in our garage. I want someone who thinks I'm the number one most important thing in their world, not number fifty or a hundred or wherever it is I fit into yours.

WAYNE: Julie—

JULIE: Do you know what that girl asked me? She asked me when I first knew I was in love. And I couldn't remember. Was I ever in love?

WAYNE: Yes, you—

JULIE: Yes, I was. I remember now. It was when we were like them. Not perfect, not without problems, but we worked them out. We held hands, we looked each other in the eye, we LIKED looking each other in the eye. When did that all go wrong, Wayne?

WAYNE: Well, I think—

JULIE: The day we got married?

WAYNE: No!—

JULIE: Or was it last night when you suddenly let me know for the first time we've spent all our money!

WAYNE: I'm always telling you we're about to spend all our money!

JULIE: You're always saying it and nothing ever happened, so why would I believe you?

WAYNE: Right, I get it! I should have let us go broke years ago, then we'd be fine!

JULIE: Marriage therapy box, Wayne! Please stick to useful suggestions! Such as why we should remain married for one more minute!

WAYNE: We're not even doing this right!

JULIE: You feel scared, Wayne? I feel scared too. You know why? Because I feel completely alone. We are not a couple, this is not a marriage. We are no longer an us. Please respond. You have sixty seconds.

WAYNE: This isn't the way they were doing it!

JULIE: What are you talking about?

WAYNE: Eyes! Give me eyes!

Almost involuntarily, she goes quiet and looks him in the eye.

Julie, you are the single most important thing in my life.

JULIE: That's the most romantic thing you've said since you told me that I was either evil or stupid.

WAYNE: I have been getting my priorities a little mixed up. Over the last ten or twenty years. The second you walked out the door I realized what my life would be without you.

JULIE: You'd be lonely without me. So get a dog.

WAYNE: I'm sorry for everything I said. I was wrong. You're right. I *am* afraid. I'm afraid of everything. And I'm a jerk. I'm an asshole. I am scum. I am not worthy of you . . .

JULIE: So tell me something I don't already know.

WAYNE: Forever, Julie.

He takes her hands.

I love you now and I will love you forever, cross my heart. Stack of Bibles, so help me god.

JULIE: No, you can't just say the same words he said, Wayne. It doesn't cost you anything. This has to hurt.

With determination, WAYNE *kneels down the way* MAGGIE *did with* JOHN, *though with a lot more difficulty.* JULIE *grudgingly follows his lead.*

Okay. That hurts.

WAYNE: The kids are right. They're arrogant little pricks, but they're right. I married you because I believed you loved me as much as I loved you and we wanted to spend the rest of our lives together. Thirty years later, we're still here. Isn't that just a little bit amazing?

JULIE: Maybe a little bit.

WAYNE: I'm proud of you, Julie. I'm proud to walk beside you, proud you're in my life, proud we made it together this long. Whatever happens next, even if you leave me, I will always know that I love you and that the most wonderful thing that ever happened to me will always be this marriage.

Pause.

JULIE: Oh . . . shitballs. This marriage is the most wonderful thing that ever happened to me too.

They kiss, then hold the hug.

I went a little crazy. I'm sorry, honey.

WAYNE: We both did. I'm sorry too, sweetheart.

JULIE: The kitchen. The marriage. We both went a little crazy together.

JULIE & WAYNE: I'm sorry, honey.

They start getting up on creaky, late-middle-age legs.

JULIE: Oh, what are we going to do, Wayne? We're broke!

WAYNE: We're not broke. We have cash flow—you still have your job.

JULIE: But that's nothing like enough!

WAYNE: We just have to spend less.

JULIE: We tried that. It doesn't work.

WAYNE: We're drowning in debt. We have to clear some of it off.

JULIE: How?

WAYNE: Option A. Declare bankruptcy.

JULIE: No.

WAYNE: If we do it, we get to keep the house, all the interest charges are gone, we can plow everything into mortgage payments—

JULIE: We are not declaring bankruptcy. What's option B?

Beat.

WAYNE: I may have thirty thousand dollars.

JULIE: You have . . . what?

WAYNE: Yeah.

JULIE: Where did you get thirty thousand dollars?

WAYNE: My severance package three years ago.

JULIE: We spent your severance package on the SUV.

WAYNE: I kind of didn't tell you about half of it.

JULIE: Where?

WAYNE: I gave it to my mother to hide in a GIC.

JULIE: Your mother is helping you hide money from your wife.

WAYNE: Only so we wouldn't spend it.

JULIE: So I wouldn't spend it, you mean.

WAYNE: I didn't say that.

JULIE: And even when we were destitute yesterday, why did you still not think you should mention it?

WAYNE & JULIE: *(simultaneously)* Same reason.

JULIE: Okay, no, wise decision. We have thirty thousand dollars, that helps.

WAYNE: We fire the kids, finish the kitchen ourselves, live like monks, cut all expenses, pay down our debts. We might even end up with a tiny retirement fund.

JULIE: Except we owe the kids thirty thousand.

WAYNE: Right. Well, obviously . . .

JULIE: What?

WAYNE: What if we don't pay them?

JULIE: You want to stiff the kids?

WAYNE: Of course I don't want to. But how many options do we have left?

JULIE: Wayne, that is disgusting! That is despicable! I can't even believe you're suggesting it!

WAYNE: I'm okay with bankruptcy, Julie. They won't get a penny either way. I am beyond dignity. My pants are three-quarters down, they might as well be at my ankles.

JULIE: They'd just take us to court.

WAYNE: Bring it on. We never even signed a contract.

JULIE: Those two penniless babes in the woods, just starting out, we'd be stealing from them!

WAYNE: Did you see the photos of their parents' kitchens? They're worth ten times our little kitchen. Mommy and Daddy will pick them up and bail them out. You know who has nothing left to fall back on? You and me.

JULIE: But they're pregnant!

WAYNE: End of our rope, Julie. We gotta tie a knot and hang on. We can make it on your salary, rebuild our lives, but it's hard choices. We can fire their asses and be done with it, just say the word.

JULIE: Who are you? I don't know you! This is not who I married! I married a good man. No matter how bad our situation is, we are not people who steal from—

But she stifles her thought, hearing JOHN *and* MAGGIE *entering from the basement.*

JOHN: Okay.

MAGGIE: So.

JOHN: Yeah.

MAGGIE: So we kind of figure, if you declare bankruptcy that leaves us pretty much screwed. But then you've got a house with no kitchen, it's worth pretty much nothing. So, we're thinking we have a win-win proposal.

WAYNE: Yeah . . . ?

JOHN: I talked to my dad, and he said he can come over evenings, no charge, and help finish the job. Which will go pretty quick if we put the wall back, drop the whole island idea, and go for the basics.

MAGGIE: We only do the stuff that gets it ready for market. You sell, we settle, we each get enough out of it that we can all go on with our lives.

JULIE: We have to sell our house.

MAGGIE: Unless you have buried treasure in the backyard.

WAYNE looks at JULIE. JULIE looks at WAYNE. WAYNE does a fearful little headshake, "No!"

JULIE: I have the most remarkable coincidence to report.

WAYNE: *(defeated)* Oh god no.

JULIE: All thirty thousand. Finish the kitchen.

MAGGIE: Certified cheque.

JULIE: Held by a third party.

MAGGIE: Eighty percent up front.

JULIE: Done.

JOHN: *(blurting)* On the condition that it's just me and my dad and I don't have to work with Wayne anymore.

WAYNE: You're firing me?

JOHN: And we want to get this done so you don't get to be in the house when we're working.

JULIE turns to WAYNE, pleased.

JULIE: We keep our home, we get back on our feet, and we are good people.

WAYNE: I'm not happy about any of this. But you're a good person, Julie. I'm proud of you.

MAGGIE *and* JOHN *hug in relief.*

JOHN: You see? They're okay.

MAGGIE: Wow. I was so wrong.

JULIE's phone rings.

JULIE: *(checking her screen)* Oh shit.
(on phone) Hi. What's up?
I called him yesterday to say I'd be taking the morning off. I
thought I'd still be able to get down there, but it got a little—
Monday morning?
Why?
No, what's it about?
Leslie, you've talked to him. You know what this is about.
No, really, tell me.
No, tell me right now.
Yeah . . . ?
I what?
I did?
They did?
They are?
Oh . . .
No comment.
No. No comment.
Yeah. I will.
I will.

She hangs up.

Pause.

WAYNE: What?

JULIE: HR wants a meeting Monday.

WAYNE: Why?

JULIE: . . . They noticed I haven't been doing any actual work for the past two weeks.

WAYNE: Well that's nothing. You were distracted. You apologize, end of story.

JULIE: And then they noticed. I did a . . . ohhhh, crap.

WAYNE: Honey? What?

JULIE: I used the company credit card to buy the dishwasher.

MAGGIE: Ohhh . . .

JULIE: I didn't mean to. The Visa was just full from the flooring. I meant to pay it back right away. I forgot.

WAYNE: Okay. Okay. There's worse things a person can do.

JULIE: *(beginning to panic)* Are there? At work?

WAYNE: Oh, much worse. I mean, how much can a dishwasher cost?

Lots apparently, from JULIE *and* MAGGIE's *faces.*

Okay, but it's just a meeting, it could be for anything.

JULIE: No, it doesn't mean they're going to fire me, right?

WAYNE: Just a slap on the wrist probably. Everything could be fine by Monday.

MAGGIE: And if it comes to it, Julie, we will work out a compromise on the billing.

JULIE: Thank you. We've come to like both of you very much.

MAGGIE: Thank you.

JOHN: We like you too.

MAGGIE: We're getting married!

JOHN: You're invited. If that's a cool thing for you.

JULIE: And we think you are awesome. Which is why this is in no way personal. I think Wayne has something to say to you.

WAYNE *inhales. Goes corporate.*

WAYNE: Thank you, Julie. And thank you both for your services.

JOHN: What . . . ?

WAYNE: Which have been greatly appreciated, but obviously economic factors beyond our control are having an impact on our operations and our hands are tied.

MAGGIE: *(to JOHN)* Oh, I fucking told you.

JOHN: Wayne, buddy—

MAGGIE: Julie? Tell us right now. Are you paying us?

JULIE: No comment.

WAYNE: As Julie said, this is in no way personal. Please pack up your tools. You have fifteen minutes to clear the premises.

JOHN: *(astonished)* Wow . . .

MAGGIE: *(not astonished)* Just, wow . . .

WAYNE: We are truly sorry. In certain environments, compassion is a luxury.

JOHN: And sometimes the dickheads can just push too far.

JOHN pulls out his cell.

Do it, Mags.

MAGGIE: You can do it.

JOHN: You read better than me.

MAGGIE: John, give yourself more credit. You have a master's in comparative literature.

JOHN: Okay, you're right.

(off his screen) "This is a picture of Julie and Wayne Matterly. Julie is an employee of the Great Midcontinental Life Assurance Company."

JULIE: Are you trying to intimidate us?

JOHN: "And this is a picture of their kitchen—before—and after my fiancée Maggie and I began renovations. And that's because

Wayne and Julie decided not to pay us. They owe us thirty thousand dollars in labour and materials. Maggie, by the way, is pregnant. We're getting married next month, and expecting in June. And thanks to Wayne and Julie—*an employee of the Great Midcontinental Life Assurance Company*—we're starting our life together with a thirty thousand dollar unrecoverable debt. So please share this post widely, so other contractors and business people, and heck, everybody, can stay clear of these horrible deadbeats."

WAYNE: So you post this and it's supposed to go viral? That's your big plan?

MAGGIE: If we wanted it to go viral we'd have put kittens in it.

> JOHN *lifts the phone.* MAGGIE *puts her finger on the screen.*

JULIE: Do not push that button! I do not like to be threatened!

MAGGIE: We're not threatening you.

WAYNE: And our lawyers don't like blackmail.

JOHN: Who's blackmailing?

WAYNE: Then what do you want?

MAGGIE: We want to get a little pickier about who we hang out with.

> MAGGIE *presses the screen. We hear the whoosh of the message being posted.*

JULIE: How many Facebook friends do you have?

JOHN: Me? Hardly use it. Couple hundred?

MAGGIE: But we tagged your company's Facebook page. And the *Free Press*. And CBC. And the *Globe and Mail*. And Twitter. Hashtag SaveJohnAndMaggie. Hashtag SaveOurBaby.

WAYNE: Oh big deal! A couple of kids whine about a job termination. Your big story is going nowhere.

JOHN: Yeah, you're probably right. But we feel better.

> *JOHN begins gathering his tools. MAGGIE's phone goes ding! And then ding! And then crazy dinging and dinging and dinging . . .*

MAGGIE: Wow. Maybe it will go a little bit viral.

> *JULIE's phone bings a text notification. She checks the screen.*

JULIE: From Leslie at work. She says "WTF?"

JOHN: Oh, that means—

JULIE: I know what it means!

> *MAGGIE's phone bings a notification. She checks the screen.*

MAGGIE: Wow. Email from Mars 100.

JOHN: What do they say?

> *She's about to open it but stops.*

MAGGIE: Nope. Not looking.

MAGGIE takes a deep breath. Drags her finger around the screen.

Putting it in the trash.

She kisses JOHN.

JOHN: Really?

He kisses her.

MAGGIE: Really really really. Times forever.

They exit, kissing. Huge gusts of wind and snow blow in. The door closes.

JULIE: We're horrible people.

WAYNE: Julie? Give me eyes.

JULIE: *(glumly)* Oh, what.

WAYNE: I can get a job. You can get a job.

JULIE: We're never going to make what we used to.

WAYNE: No, but so what. Maybe we can find something we like doing. Or not. I don't care. I want to go back to work.

JULIE: For the rest of our lives we will be the two people who invited a smart, young, engaged pregnant couple into our house and stole thirty thousand dollars from them. I'm not proud of us, Wayne.

WAYNE: We're broke, and we're still together. Aren't we?

JULIE: Yes. We are.

WAYNE: Then good enough.

He grabs his phone, starts texting.

JULIE looks over his shoulder.

JULIE: What are you doing?

WAYNE: Texting her.

JULIE: Why?

WAYNE: Because she won't listen to a voice message from me, but she can't help reading a text.

JULIE: *(off WAYNE's phone)* "I'm sorry. We were wrong and we'd like to fix it. Can we talk?" Where'd you learn to do that?

WAYNE: Read your messages some day.

He presses send. It makes the whooshing sound.

How much did they really put up for costs?

JULIE: Seventeen thousand dollars for the cabinets. Three thousand for the flooring.

WAYNE: You gave them three thousand for the flooring, right?

JULIE: Right.

WAYNE: So just the seventeen thousand. We paid them twenty percent up front—so take six thousand dollars off, leaves eleven thousand still owed, add maybe a grand in smaller stuff, makes twelve—

There's an incoming text notification sound.

She answered! Says, "What." Good start.

Add two weeks' work—to be very generous, say sixteen thousand all told?

JULIE: They said we owed them thirty.

WAYNE: Bluffing.

JULIE: You're actually paying them after that?

WAYNE: Losing the killer instinct, I guess.

(texting) I'm offering fourteen thousand.

JULIE: Oh, make it sixteen.

WAYNE: Fifteen.

JULIE: Sold.

Whoosh. They wait. Like parents texting their twelve-year-old for the first time, waiting for an answer.

An incoming notification sound.

What what what?

WAYNE: "Holy crap. For real?"

WAYNE texts. Whoosh!

JULIE: What'd you say?

WAYNE: Bible.

JULIE: What?

WAYNE: It's a Kim Kardashian thing. You wouldn't know.

Incoming notification sound.

"Dude. Hashtag Wasn'tExpectingThat. Hashtag Respect. Hashtag ProudOfYou."

(speaks while texting) "Hashtag Can'tEatMoney."

Whoosh!

JULIE: Look at you. You're never going to talk on the phone again.

WAYNE: Who does?

(an afterthought, speaking as he texts) "Does John want to come back and finish kitchen with me?"

Whoosh!

JULIE: *(excited)* Oh!

Incoming notification sound.

WAYNE: *(off his phone)* Hashtag UpYours. Dagger. Gun. Coffin. I think the wedding invitation's off.

JULIE: They do hate us.

WAYNE: Maybe not completely. Smiley Poop!

JULIE: I'm proud of you too, Wayne.

WAYNE: Thank you, my love.

JULIE: Doing anything for the rest of your life?

WAYNE: Yup. Hashtag You.

They kiss, lean back against the cripple wall like a couple of necking teenagers. Plaster begins to fall. Cracking sounds.

JULIE: Should we worry about that?

WAYNE: Nope.

They keep necking. More plaster falls on their heads as the cracking sounds grow louder and the ceiling collapses. They don't notice. Lights spark, flash, go out.

The end.

ACKNOWLEDGEMENTS

I again owe huge gratitude to Robert Metcalfe for his unending support as a friend, dramaturg, and director of this play. Thanks as well to the brilliant cast, designers, and crew of the original production at Prairie Theatre Exchange, and always to the PTE Playwrights Unit.

The writing and development of this play was generously supported by a grant from the Canada Council for the Arts.

Rick Chafe's plays include Governor General's Literary Award finalist *The Secret Mask*, *Shakespeare's Dog* (adapted from the novel by Leon Rooke), *Strike!* and its film adaptation *Stand!* (both co-written with Danny Schur), *Red Earth* (co-written with Kristian Jordan), *Beowulf*, and *The Odyssey*. Rick lives in Winnipeg with his wife, Martine; their daughter, Charlotte; two cats; and their new kitchen.

First edition: June 2019
Printed and bound in Canada by Rapido Books, Montreal

Jacket design by Kisscut Design

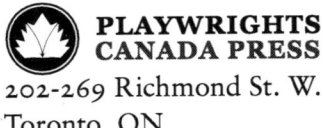

**PLAYWRIGHTS
CANADA PRESS**
202-269 Richmond St. W.
Toronto, ON
M5V 1X1

416.703.0013
info@playwrightscanada.com
www.playwrightscanada.com
@playcanpress